THE

ORBIS PICTUS

OF

JOHN AMOS COMENIUS.

This work is, indeed, the first children's picture book.—
ENCYCLOPÆDIA BRITANNICA, 9TH EDITION, vi. 182.

SYRACUSE, N. Y.:
C. W. BARDEEN, PUBLISHER,
1887.

Now Reissued by
Singing Tree Press
1249 Washington Blvd., Detroit, Michigan 1968

It may not be generally known that Comenius was once solicited to become President of Harvard College. The following is a quotation from Vol. II, p. 14, of Cotton Mather's MAGNALIA:

"That brave old man, Johannes Amos Commenius, the fame of whose worth has been TRUMPETTED as far as more than three languages (whereof everyone is indebted unto his JANUA) could carry it, was indeed agreed withal, by one Mr. Winthrop in his travels through the LOW COUNTRIES, to come over to New England, and illuminate their Colledge and COUNTRY, in the quality of a President, which was now become vacant. But the solicitations of the Swedish Ambassador diverting him another way, that incomparable Moravian became not an American."

This was on the resignation of President Dunster, in 1654 — NOTE OF PROF. PAYNE, COMPAYRE'S HISTORY OF EDUCATION, BOSTON, 1886, P. 125.

Library of Congress Catalog Card Number 67—23933

EDITOR'S PREFACE.

When it is remembered that this work is not only an educational classic of prime importance, but that it was the first picture-book ever made for children and was for a century the most popular text-book in Europe, and yet has been for many years unattainable on account of its rarity, the wonder is, not that it is reproduced now but that it has not been reproduced before. But the difficulty has been to find a satisfactory copy. Many as have been the editions, few copies have been preserved. It was a book children were fond of and wore out in turning the leaves over and over to see the pictures. Then as the old copper-plates became indistinct they were replaced by wood-engravings, of coarse execution, and often of changed treatment. Von Raumer complains that the edition of 1755 substitutes for the original cut of the Soul, *(*No. 43, as here given,*)* a picture of an eye, and in a table the figures I. I. II. I. I. II., and adds that it is difficult to recognize in this an expressive psychological symbol, and to explain it. In an edition I have, published in Vienna in 1779, this cut is omitted altogether, and indeed there are but 82 in place of the 157 found in earlier editions, the following, as numbered in this edition, being omitted:

1, the alphabet, 2, 36, 43, 45, 66, 68, 75, 76, 78–80, 87, 88, 92–122, 124, 126, 128, 130–141.

On the other hand, the Vienna edition contains a
curious additional cut. It gives No. 4, the Heaven,
practically as in this edition, but puts another cut
under it in which the earth is revolving about the
sun; and after the statement of Comenius, *"Coelum ro-
tatur, et ambit terram, in medio stantem"* interpolates:
*"prout veteres crediderunt; recentiores enim defendunt
motum terrae circa solem"* [as the ancients used to think;
for later authorities hold that the motion of the earth
is about the sun.]

Two specimen pages from another edition are inserted in Payne's Compayré's History of Education
(between pp. 126, 127). The cut is the representa-
tive of No. 103 in this edition, but those who com-
pare them will see not only how much coarser is the
execution of the wood-cut Prof. Payne has copied,
but what liberties have been taken with with the design. The only change in the Latin text, however,
is from *Designat Figuras rerum* in the original, to
Figuram rerum designat.

In this edition the cuts are unusually clear copies
of the copper-plates of the first edition of 1658, from
which we have also taken the Latin text. The text
for the English translation is from the English edition of 1727, in which for the first time the English
words were so arranged as to stand opposite their
Latin equivalents.

The cuts have been reproduced with great care by
the photographic process. I thought best not to per-
mit them to be retouched, preferring occasional in-
distinctness to modern tampering with the originals
that would make them less authentic.

The English text is unchanged from that of the 1727 edition, except in rare instances where substitutions have been made for single words not now permissible. The typography suggests rather than imitates the quaintness of the original, and the paper was carefully selected to produce so far as practicable the impression of the old hand-presses.

In short my aim has been to put within the reach of teachers at a moderate price a satisfactory reproduction of this important book; and if the sale of the *Orbis Pictus* seems to warrant it, I hope subsequently to print as a companion volume the *Vestibulum* and *Janua* of the same author, of which I have choice copies.   C. W. BARDEEN.

Syracuse, Sept. 28, 1887.

Comments upon the Orbis Pictus.

During four years he here prosecuted his efforts in behalf of education with commendable success, and wrote, among other works, his celebrated Orbis Pictus, which has passed through a great many editions, and survived a multitude of imitations.—Smith's History of Education, N. Y., 1842, p. 129.

The most eminent educator of the seventeenth century, however, was John Amos Comenius......His Orbis Sensualium Pictus, published in 1657, enjoyed a still higher renown. The text was much the same with the Janua, being intended as a kind of elementary encyclopædia; but *it differed from all previous text-books*, in being illustrated with pictures, on copper and wood, of the various topics discussed in it. This book was universally popular. In those portions of Germany where the schools had been broken up by the "Thirty years' war," mothers taught their children from its pages. Corrected and amended by later editors, it continued for nearly two hundred years, to be a text-book of the German schools.— History and Progress of Education, by Philobiblius, N. Y., 1860, p. 210.

The "Janua" would, therefore, have had but a short-lived popularity with teachers, and a still shorter with learners, if Comenius had not carried out his principle of appealing to the senses, and called in the artist. The result was the "Orbis Pictus," a book which proved a favorite with young and old, and maintained its ground in many a school for more than a century....I am sorry I cannot give a specimen of this celebrated book with its quaint pictures. The artist, of course, was wanting in the technical skill which is now commonly displayed even in the cheapest publications, but this renders his delineations none the less entertaining. As a picture of the life and manners of the seventeeth century, the work has great historical interest, which will, I hope, secure for it another English edition.—QUICK's EDUCATIONAL REFORMERS, 1868; Syracuse edition, p. 79.

But the principle on which he most insisted is that the teaching of words and things must go together, hand in hand. When we consider how much time is spent over new languages, what waste of energy is lavished on mere preparation, how it takes so long to lay a foundation that there is no time to lay a building upon it, we must conclude that it is in the acceptance and development of this principle that the improvement of education will in the future consist. Any one who attempts to inculcate this great reform will find that its first principles are contained in the writings of Comenius.—ENCYCLOPAEDIA BRITANNICA, 9th edition, vii. 674.

The first edition of this celebrated book was published at Nuremberg in 1657; soon after a translation was made into English by Charles Hoole. The last English edition appeared in 1777, and this was reprinted in America in 1812. This was the first il-

lustrated school-book, and was the first attempt at
what now passes under the name of "object lessons."
—SHORT HISTORY OF EDUCATION, W. H. PAYNE, Syracuse, 1881, p. 103.

Of these, the "Janua" and the "Orbis" were translated into most European and some of the Oriental
languages. It is evident that these practices of Comenius contain the germs of things afterwards con-
nected with the names of Pestalozzi and Stow. It
also may be safely assumed that many methods that
are now in practical use, were then not unknown to
earliest teachers.—GILL'S SYSTEMS OF EDUCATION,
London, 1876, p. 13.

The more we reflect on the method of Comenius,
the more we shall see it is replete with suggestive-
ness, and we shall feel surprised that so much wisdom can have lain in the path of schoolmasters for
two hundred and fifty years, and that they have never
stooped to avail themselves of its treasures.—BROWN-
ING'S INTRODUCTION TO THE HISTORY OF EDUCATIONAL
THEORIES, 1882, New York edition, p. 67.

The "Orbis Pictus," the first practical application
of the intuitive method, had an extraordinary success, and has served as a model for the innumerable
illustrated books which for three centuries have in-
vaded the schools.—COMPAYRE'S HISTORY OF PEDA-
GOGY, Payne's translation, Boston, 1886, p. 127.

He remained at Patak four years, which were char-
acterized by surprising literary activity. During
this short period he produced no less than fifteen
different works, among them his "World Illustrated"
(*Orbis Pictus*), the most famous of all his writings.

It admirably applied the principle that words and things should be learned together....The "World Illustrated" had an enormous circulation, and remained for a long time the most popular text-book in Europe.—PAINTER'S HISTORY OF EDUCATION, N.Y., 1886, p. 206.

Or, si ce livre n'est qu'un equivalent le la véritable intuition; si, ensuite, le contenu du tout paraît fort defectueux, au point de vue de la science de nos jours; si, enfin, un effort exagéré pour l' integrité de la conception de l' enfant a créé, pour les choses modernes, trop de dénominations latines qui paraissent douteuses, l' *Orbis pictus* était pourtant, pour son temps, une oeuvre très originale et très spirituelle, qui fit faire un grand progrès à la pedagogie et servit longtemps de livre d' ecole utile et de modèle á d' innomorables livres d' images, souvent pires.—HISTORIE D'ÉDUCATION, FREDERICK DITTES, Redolfi's French translation, Paris, 1880, p. 178.

Here Comenius wrote, among others, his second celebrated work the "Orbis Pictus." He was not, however, able to finish it in Hungary for want of a skilful engraver on copper. For such a one he carried it to Michael Endter, the bookseller at Nuremberg, but the engraving delayed the publication of the book for three years more. In 1657 Comenius expressed the hope that it would appear during the next autumn. With what great approbation the work was received at its first appearance, is shown by the fact that within two years, in 1659, Endter had published a second enlarged edition.—KARL VON

Raumer, translated in Barnard's Journal of Education, v. 260.

The "Janua" had an enormous sale, and was published in many languages, but the editions and sale of the "Orbis Pictus" far exceeded those of the "Janua," and, indeed, for some time it was the most popular text-book in Europe, and deservedly so.— Laurie's John Amos Comenius, Boston edition, p. 185.

Joh. Amos Comenii
Orbis Sensualium Pictus:
HOC EST

Omnium principalium in Mundo
Rerum, & in Vita Actionum,

Pictura & Nomenclatura.

Joh. Amos Comenius's
VISIBLE WORLD:
OR, A

Nomenclature, and Pictures
OF ALL THE

Chief Things that are in the World, and
of Mens Employments therein;

In above 150 Copper Cuts.

WRITTEN

By the Author in Latin and High Dutch, being
one of his last Essays; and the most suitable to Childrens Capacity of any he hath hitherto made.

Translated into English

By Charles Hoole, M. A.

For the Use of Young Latin Scholars.

The Eleventh Edition Corrected, and the English made to
answer Word for Word to the Latin.

Nihil est in intellectu, quod non prius fuit in sensu. Arist.

London; Printed for, and sold by *John* and *Benj.
Sprint,* at the *Bell* in *Little Britain,* 1728.

Gen. ii. 19, 20.

The Lord God brought unto *Adam* every Beast of the Field, and every Fowl of the Air, to see what he would call them. And *Adam* gave Names to all Cattle, and to the Fowl of the Air, and to every Beast of the Field.

Gen. ii. 19, 20.

Adduxit Dominus Deus ad Adam *cuncta Animantia Terræ, & universa volatilia Cœli, ut videret quomodo vocaret illa. Appellavitque* Adam *Nominibus suis cuncta Animantia, & universa volatilia Cœli, & omnes Bestias Agri.*

I. A. Comenii opera Didactica par. 1. p. 6, Amst. 1657. fol.

Didacticæ nostræ prora & puppis esto : Investigare, & invenire modum, quo Docentes minus doceant, Discentes vero plus discant : Scholæ minus habeant Strepitus, nauseæ, vani laboris ; plus autem otii, deliciarum, solidique profectus : Respublica Christiana minus tenebrarum confusionis dissidiorum ; plus lucis, ordinis, pacis & tranquilitatis.

The Author's Preface to the Reader.

Instruction is the means to expel Rudeness, with which young wits ought to be well furnished in Schools: But so, as that the teaching be 1. *True*, 2. *Full*, 3. *Clear*, and 4. *Solid*.

1. It will be *true*, if nothing be taught but such as is beneficial to ones life; lest there be a cause of complaining afterwards. We know not necessary things, because we have not learned things necessary.

2. It will be *full*, if the mind be polished for wisdom, the tongue for eloquence, and the hands for a neat way of living. This will be that *grace* of one's life, *to be wise, to act, to speak*.

3, 4. It will be *clear*, and by that, firm and *solid*, if whatever is taught and learned, be not obscure, or confused, but apparent, distinct, and articulate, as the fingers on the hands.

The ground of this business, is, that sensual objects may be rightly presented to the senses, for fear they may not be received. I say, and say it again aloud, that this last is the foundation of all the rest: because we can neither act nor speak wisely, unless we first rightly understand all the things which are to be done, and whereof we are to speak. Now there is nothing in the understanding, which was not before in the sense. And therefore to exercise the senses well about the right perceiving the differences of things, will be to lay the grounds for all wisdom, and all wise discourse, and all discreet actions in ones course of life. Which, because it is commonly neglected in schools, and the things which are to be learned are offered to scholars, without being understood or being rightly presented to the senses, it cometh to pass, that the work of teaching and learning goeth heavily onward, and affordeth little benefit.

See here then a new help for schools, A Picture and Nomenclature of all the chief things in the world, and of men's actions in their way of living: Which, that you, good Masters, may not be loath to run over with your scholars, I will tell you, in short, what good you may expect from it.

It is *a little Book*, as you see, of no great bulk, yet a brief of the whole world, and a whole language: full of Pictures, Nomenclatures, and Descriptions of things.

i. *The Pictures* are the representation of all visible things, (to which also things invisible are reduced after their fashion) of the whole world. And that in that very order of things, in which they are described in the *Janua Latinæ Linguæ;* and with that fulness, that nothing very necessary or of great concernment is omitted.

II. *The Nomenclatures* are the Inscriptions, or Titles set every one over their own Pictures, expressing the whole thing by its own general term.

III. *The Descriptions* are the explications of the parts of the Picture, so expressed by their own proper terms, as that same figure which is added to every piece of the picture, and the term of it, always sheweth what things belongeth one to another.

Which such Book, and in such a dress may (I hope) serve,

I. To entice witty children to it, that they may not conceit a torment to be in the school, but dainty fare. For it is apparent, that children (even from their infancy almost) are delighted with Pictures, and willingly please their eyes with these lights: And it will be very well worth the pains to have once brought it to pass, that scare-crows may be taken away out of Wisdom's Gardens.

II. This same little Book will serve to stir up the Attention, which is to be fastened upon things, and even to be sharpened more and more: which is also a great matter. For the Senses (being the main guides of childhood, because therein the mind doth not as yet raise up itself to an abstracted contemplation of things) evermore seek their own objects, and if they be away, they grow dull, and wry themselves hither and thither out of a weariness of themselves: but when their objects are present, they grow merry, wax lively, and willingly suffer themselves to be fastened upon them, till the thing be sufficiently discerned. This Book then will do a good piece of service in taking (especially flickering) wits, and preparing them for deeper studies.

III. Whence a third good will follow; that children being won hereunto, and drawn over with this

way of heeding, may be furnished with the knowledge of the prime things that are in the world, by
sport and merry pastime.   In a word, this Book will
serve for the more pleasing using of the *Vestibulum*
and *Janua Linguarum*, for which end it was even at
the first chiefly intended.   Yet if it like any, that it
be bound up in their native tongues also, it prom-
iseth three good thing of itself.

I. First it will afford a device for learning to read
more easily than hitherto, especially having a sym-
bolical alphabet set before it, to wit, the characters
of the several letters, with the image of that creature,
whose voice that letter goeth about to imitate, pic-
tur'd by it.   For the young *Abc* scholar will easily
remember the force of every character by the very
looking upon the creature, till the imagination being
strengthened by use, can readily afford all things;
and then having looked over *a table of the chief sylla-
bles* also *(*which yet was not thought necessary to be
added to this book*)* he may proceed to the viewing
of the Pictures, and the inscriptions set over 'em.
Where again the very looking upon the thing pictured suggesting the name of the thing, will tell him
how the title of the picture is to be read.   And
thus the whole book being gone over by the bare
titles of the pictures, reading cannot but be learned ;
and indeed too, which thing is to be noted, without
using any ordinary tedious spelling, that most trouble-
some torture of wits, which may wholly be avoided
by this method.   For the often reading over the
Book, by those larger descriptions of things, and
which are set after the Pictures, will be able perfectly to beget a habit of reading.

II. The same book being used in English, in English Schools, will serve for the perfect learning of the whole English tongue, and that from the bottom; because by the aforesaid descriptions of things, the words and phrases of the whole language are found set orderly in their own places. And a short English Grammar might be added at the end, clearly resolving the speech already understood into its parts; shewing the declining of the several words, and reducing those that are joined together under certain rules.

III. Thence a new benefit cometh, that that very English Translation may serve for the more ready and pleasant learning of the Latin tongue : as one may see in this Edition, the whole book being so translated, that every where one word answereth to the word over against it, and the book is in all things the same, only in two idioms, as a man clad in a double garment. And there might be also some observations and advertisements added in the end, touching those things only, wherein the use of the Latin tongue differeth from the English. For where there is no difference, there needeth no advertisement to be given. But, because the first *tasks of learners ought to be little and single*, we have filled this first book of training one up to see a thing of himself, with nothing but rudiments, that is, with the chief of things and words, or with the grounds of the whole world, and the whole language, and of all our understanding about things. If a more perfect description of things, and a fuller knowledge of a language, and a clearer light of the understanding be

B

sought after *(*as they ought to be*)* they are to be found somewhere whither there will now be an easy passage by this our *little Encyclopædia* of things subject to the senses.   Something remaineth to be said touching the more chearful use of this book.

I. Let it be given to children into their hands to delight themselves withal as they please, with the sight of the pictures, and making them as familiar to themselves as may be, and that even at home before they be put to school.

II. Then let them be examined ever and anon *(*especially now in the school*)* what this thing or that thing is, and is called, so that they may see nothing which they know not how to name, and that they can name nothing which they cannot shew.

III. And let the things named them be shewed, not only in the Picture, but also in themselves; for example, the parts of the body, clothes, books, the house, utensils, *&c.*

IV. Let them be suffered also to imitate the Pictures by hand, if they will, nay rather, let them be encouraged, that they may be willing : first, thus to quicken the attention also towards the things; and to observe the proportion of the parts one towards another ; and lastly to practise the nimbleness of the hand, which is good for many things.

V. If anything here mentioned, cannot be presented to the eye, it will be to no purpose at all to offer them by themselves to the scholars; as colours, relishes, *&c.*, which cannot here be pictured out with ink.   For which reason it were to be wished, that things rare and not easy to be met withal at home, might be kept ready in every great school, that they may be shewed also, as often as any words are to be made of them, to the scholars.

Thus at last this school would indeed become a school of things obvious to ,the senses, and an entrance to the school intellectual. But enough : Let us come to the thing it self.

The Translator, to all judicious and industrious School-Masters.

———

Gentlemen.

There are a few of you (I think) but have seen, and with great willingness made use of (or at least perused,) many of the Books of this of this well-deserving Author Mr. John Comenius, which for their profitableness to the speedy attainment of a language, have been translated in several countries, out of Latin into their own native tongue.

Now the general verdict (after trial made) that hath passed, touching those formerly extant, is this, that they are indeed of singular use, and very advantageous to those of more discretion, (especially to such as already have a smattering of Latin) to help their memories to retain what they have scatteringly gotten here and there, to furnish them with many words, which (perhaps) they had not formerly read, or so well observed; but to young children (whom we have chiefly to instruct) as those that are ignorant altogether of things and words, and prove rather a meer toil and burthen, than a delight and furtherance.

For to pack up many words in memory, of things not conceived in the mind, is to fill the head with empty imaginations, and to make the learner more to admire the multitude and variety *(*and thereby, to become discouraged,*)* than to care to treasure them up, in hopes to gain more knowledge of what they mean.

He hath therefore in some of his latter works seemed to move retrograde, and striven to come nearer the reach of tender wits : and in this present Book, he hath, according to my judgment, descended to the very bottom of what is to be taught, and proceeded *(*as nature it self doth*)* in an orderly way; first to exercise the senses well, by representing their objects to them, and then to fasten upon the intellect by impressing the first notions of things upon it, and linking them on to another by a rational discourse. Whereas indeed, we, generally missing this way, do teach children as we do parrots, to speak they know not what, nay which is worse, we, taking the way of teaching little ones by Grammar only at the first, do puzzle their imaginations with abstractive terms and secondary intentions, which till they be somewhat acquainted with things, and the words belonging to them, in the language which they learn, they cannot apprehend what they mean.   And this I guess to be the reason, why many great persons do resolve sometimes not to put a child to school till he be at least eleven or twelve years of age, presuming that he having then taken notice of most things, will sooner get the knowledge of the words which are applyed to them in any language.   But the gross misdemeanor of such children for the most part, have taught many parents to be hasty enough to send their own to school, if not that they may learn, yet *(*at least*)* that they might be kept out of harm's way; and yet if they do not profit for the time they have been at school, (no respect at all being had for their years) the Master shall be sure enough to bear the blame.

So that a School-master had need to bend his wits to come within the compass of a child's capacity of six or seven years of age (seeing we have now such commonly brought to our Grammar-schools to learn the Latin Tongue) and to make that they may learn with as much delight and willingness, as himself would teach with dexterity and ease. And at present I know no better help to forward his young scholars than this little Book, which was for this purpose contrived by the Author in the German and Latin Tongues.

What profitable use may be had thereof, respecting chiefly that his own country and language, he himself hath told you in his preface; but what use we may here make of it in our Grammar-schools, as it is now translated into English, I shall partly declare; leaving all other men, according to my wont, to their own discretion and liberty, to use or refuse it, as they please. So soon then as a child can read English perfectly, and is brought to us to school to learn Latin, I would have him together with his Accidence, to be provided of this Book, in which he may at least once a day (beside his Accidence) be thus exercised.

I. Let him look over the pictures with their general titles and inscriptions, till he be able to turn readily to any one of them, and to tell its name either in English or Latin. By this means he shall have the method of the Book in his head; and be easily furnished with the knowledge of most things; and instructed how to call them, when at any time he meeteth with them elsewhere, in their real forms.

II. Let him read the description at large: First in English, and afterward in Latin, till he can readily read, and distinctly pronounce the words in both Languages, ever minding how they are spelled. And withal, let him take notice of the figures inserted, and to what part of the picture they direct by their like till he be well able to find out every particular thing of himself, and to name it on a sudden, either in English or Latin.   Thus he shall not only gain the most primitive words, but be understandingly grounded in Orthography, which is a thing too generally neglected by us; partly because our English schools think that children should learn it at the Latin, and our Latin schools suppose they have already learn'd it at the English; partly, because our common Grammar is too much defective in this part, and scholars so little exercised therein, that they pass from schools to the Universities and return from thence (some of them) more unable to write true English, than either Latin or Greek.   Not to speak of our ordinary Tradesmen, many of whom write such false English, that none but themselves can interpret what they scribble in their bills and shop-books.

III. Then let him get the Titles and Descriptions by heart, which he will more easily do, by reason of these impressions which the viewing of the pictures hath already made in his memory.   And now let him also learn, 1. To construe, or give the words one by

one, as they answer one another in Latin and English. 2. To Parse, according to the rules, *(*which I
presume by this time*)* he hath learn'd in the first
part of his Accidence; where I would have him tell
what part of Speech any word is, and then what ac-
cidents belong to it; but especially to decline the
nouns and conjugate the verbs according to the Ex-
amples in his Rudiments; and this doing will enable
him to know the end and use of his Accidence. As
for the Rules of Genders of Nouns, and the Præter-
perfect-tenses and Supines of Verbs, and those of
Concordance and Construction in the latter part of
the Accidence, I would not have a child much
troubled with them, till by the help of this Book he
can perfectly practise so much of Etymology, as con-
cerns the first part of his Accidence only. For that,
and this book together, being thoroughly learn'd by
at least thrice going them over, will much prepare
children to go chearfully forward in their Grammar
and School-Authors, especially, if whilst they are
employed herein, they be taught also to write a fair
and legible hand.

There is one thing to be given notice of, which I
wish could have been remedied in this Translation;
that the Book being writ in high-Dutch doth express
many things in reference to that Country and Speech,
which cannot without alteration of some Pictures as
well as words be expressed in ours: for the Symbol-
ical Alphabet is fitted for German children rather
than for ours. And whereas the words of that Language go orderly one for one with the Latin, our
English propriety of Speech will not admit the like.
Therefore it will behove those Masters that intend

to make use of this Book, to construe it verbatim to
their young Scholars, who will quickly learn to do
it of themselves, after they be once acquainted with
the first words of Nouns, and Verbs, and their manner of variation.

Such a work as this, I observe to have been formerly much desired by some experienced Teachers,
and I my self had some years since (whilst my own
Child lived) begun the like, having found it most
agreeable to the best witted Children, who are most
taken up with Pictures from their Infancy, because
by them the knowledge of things which they seem to
represent (and whereof Children are as yet ignorant) are most easily conveyed to the Understanding.
But for as much as the work is now done, though in
some things not so completely as it were to be wished,
I rejoyce in the use of it, and desist in my own under-
takings for the present. And because any good thing
is the better, being the more communicated ; I have
herein imitated a Child who is forward to impart to
others what himself has well liked. You then that
have the care of little Children, do not much trouble
their thoughts and clog their memories with bare
Grammar Rudiments, which to them are harsh in
getting, and fluid in retaining ; because indeed to
them they signifie nothing, but a mere swimming
notion of a general term, which they know not what
it meaneth, till they comprehend particulars, but by
this or the like subsidiary, inform them, first with
some knowledge of things and words wherewith to
express them, and then their Rules of speaking will
be better understood and more firmly kept in mind.
Else how should a Child conceive what a Rule mean-

eth, when he neither knoweth what the Latin word im-
porteth, nor what manner of thing it is which is sig-
nified to him in his own native Language, which is
given him thereby to understand the Rule? For
Rules consisting of generalities, are delivered (as I
may say) at a third hand, presuming first the things,
and then the words to be already apprehended touching which they are made. I might indeed enlarge
upon this Subject, it being the very Basis of our Profession, to search into the way of Childrens taking
hold by little and little of what we teach them, that
so we may apply ourselves to their reach: But I
leave the observation thereof to your own daily exercise, and experience got thereby.

And I pray God, the fountain and giver of all wisdom, that hath bestowed upon us this gift of Teaching, so to inspire and direct us by his Grace, that
we may train up Children in his Fear and in the
knowledge of his Son Jesus Christ our Lord; and
then no doubt our teaching and their learning of other
things subordinate to these, will by the assistance of
his blessed Spirit make them able and willing to do
him faithful Service both in Church and Common-
wealth, as long as they live here, that so they may be
eternally blessed with him hereafter. This, I beseech
you, beg for me and mine, as I shall daily do for
you and yours, at the throne of God's heavenly grace;
and remain while I live

  Ready to serve you, as I truly love and honour you,
   and labour willingly in the same Profession with
   you,   CHARLES HOOLE.
From my School, in
   Lothbury, London, Jan. 25, 1658.

N. B. Those Heads or Descriptions which concern things beyond the present apprehension of Children's wits, as, those of Geography, Astronomy, or the like, I would have omitted, till the rest be learned, and a Child be *better able to understand them.*

The Judgment of Mr. Hezekiah Woodward, *sometimes an* eminent Schoolmaster in LONDON, *touching a work of this Nature ; in his* Gate to Science, *chap.* 2.

Certainly *the use of Images or Representations is great :* If we could make our words as legible to Children as Pictures are, their information therefrom would be quickned and surer. But so we cannot do, though we must do what we can. And if we had Books, wherein are the Pictures of all Creatures, Herbs, Beasts, Fish, Fowls, they would stand us in great stead. For Pictures are the most intelligible Books that Children can look upon. They come closest to Nature, nay, saith Scaliger, Art exceeds her.

AN ADVERTISEMENT CONCERNING THIS EDITION.

———

AS there are some considerable Alterations in the present Edition of this Book from the former, it may be expected an Account should be given of the Reasons for them. 'Tis certain from the Author's Words, that when it was first published, which was in Latin and Hungary, or in Latin and High-Dutch; every where one word answer'd to an-other over-against it :   This might have been observ'd in our English Translation, which wou'd have fully answer'd the design of COMENIUS, and have made the Book much more useful: But Mr. Hoole, (whether out of too much scrupulousness to disturb the Words in some places from the order they were in, or not sufficiently considering the Inconveniences of having the Latin and English so far asunder) has made them so much disagree, that a Boy has sometimes to seek 7 or 8 lines off for the corresponding Word ; which is no small trouble to Young Learners who are at first equally unacquainted with all Words, in a Lan-guage they are strangers to, except it be such as have Figures of Reference, or are very like in sound ; and thus may perhaps, innocently enough join an Adverb in one Tongue, to a Noun in the other ; whence m ay

(xxviii)

appear the Necessity of the Translation's being exactly literal, and the two Languages fairly answering one another, Line for Line.

If it be objected, such a thing cou'd not be done (considering the difference of the Idioms) without transplacing Words here and there, and putting them into an order which may not perhaps be exactly classical; it ought to be observed, this is design'd for Boys chiefly, or those who are just entering upon the Latin Tongue, to whom every thing ought to be made as plain and familiar as possible, who are not, at their first beginning, to be taught the elegant placing of Latin, nor from such short Sentences as these, but from Discourses where the Periods have a fuller Close. Besides, this way has already taken (according to the Advice of very good Judges,) in some other School-Books of Mr. Hoole's translating, and found to succeed abundantly well.

Such Condescensions as these, to the capacities of young Learners are certainly very reasonable, and wou'd be most agreeable to the Intentions of the Ingenious and worthy Author, and his design to suit whatever he taught, to their manner of apprehending it. Whose Excellency in the art of Education made him so famous all over Europe, as to be solicited by several States and Princes to go and reform the Method of their Schools; and whose works carried that Esteem, that in his own Life-time some part of them were not only translated into 12 of the usual Languages of Europe, but also into the *Arabic*, *Turkish*, *Persian*, and *Mogolic* (the common Tongue of all that part of the *East-Indies*) and since his death, into

the *Hebrew*, and some others. Nor did they want
their due Encouragement here in *England*, some Years
ago; 'till by an indiscreet use of them, and want of a
thorow acquaintance with his Method, or unwilling-
ness to part from their old road, they began to be
almost quite left off: Yet it were heartily to be
wish'd, some Persons of Judgment and Interest,
whose Example might have an influence upon others,
and bring them into Reputation again, wou'd revive
the COMENIAN METHOD, which is no other, than
to make our Scholars learn with Delight and chear-
fulness, and to convey a solid and useful Knowledge
of Things, with that of Languages, in an easy, natural
and familiar way. *Didactic Works* (as they are now
collected into one volume) for a speedy attaining the
Knowledge of Things and Words, join'd with the
Discourses of Mr. Lock* and 2 or 3 more out of our
own Nation, for forming the Mind and settling good
Habits, may doubtless be look'd upon to contain the
most reasonable, orderly, and completed System of
the Art of Education, that can be met with.

Yet, alas ! how few are there, who follow the way
they have pointed out ? tho' every one who seriously
considers it, must be convinc'd of the Advantage ;
and the generality of Schools go on in the same old
dull road, wherein a great part of Children's time is
lost in a tiresome heaping up a Pack of dry and un-
profitable, or pernicious Notions (for surely little

*Mr. Lock's Essay upon Education.
Dr. Tabor's Christain Schoolmaster.
Dr. Ob. Walker of Education.
Mr. Monro's Essay on Education.
—His just Measures of the pious Institutions of Youth, &c

better can be said of a great part of that Heathenish
stuff they are tormented with ; like the feeding them
with hard Nuts, which when they have almost broke
their teeth with cracking, they find either deaf or to
contain but very rotten and unwholesome Kernels)
whilst Things really perfected of the understanding,
and useful in every state of Life, are left unregarded,
to the Reproach of our Nation, where all other Arts
are improved and flourish well, only this of Education of Youth is at a stand ; as if that, the good or ill
management of which is of the utmost consequence
to all, were a thing not worth any Endeavors to im-
prove it, or was already so perfect and well executed
that it needed none, when many of the greatest
Wisdom and Judgment in several Nations, have with
a just indignation endeavor'd to expose it, and to
establish a more easy and useful way in its room.

'Tis not easy to say little on so important a subject,
but thus much may suffice for the present purpose.
The Book has merit enough to recommend it self to
those who know how to make a right use of it. It was
reckon'd one of the Author's best performances ; and
besides the many Impressions and Translations it has
had in parts beyond Sea, has been several times reprinted here. It was endeavor'd no needless Alterations shou'd be admitted in this Edition, and as little
of any as cou'd consist with the design of making it
plain and useful ; to shun the offence it might give
to some ; and only the Roman and Italic Character
alternately made use of, where transplacing of Words
cou'd be avoided.

London,   J. H.
July 13, 1727.

Orbis Sensualium Pictus,

A World of Things Obvious to the Senses drawn in Pictures.

Invitation.   I.   Invitatio.

The Master and the Boy. | *Magister & Puer.*

M. Come, Boy, learn to be wise.

P. What doth this mean, *to be wise?*

M. To understand rightly,

M. Veni, Puer, disce sapere.

P. Quid hoc est, *Sapere?*

M. Intelligere recte,

to do rightly, and to speak out rightly all that are necessary.

P. Who will teach me this?

M. I, by God's help.

P. How?

M. I will guide thee thorow all.

I will shew thee all.

I will name thee all.

P. See, here I am; lead me in the name of God.

M. Before all things, thou oughtest to learn the plain *sounds*, of which man's *speech* consisteth; which *living creatures* know how *to make*, and thy *Tongue* knoweth how *to imitate*, and thy *hand* can *picture out*.

Afterwards we will go into the *World*, and we will view all things.

Here thou hast a lively and Vocal Alphabet.

agere recte, et eloqui recte omnia necessaria.

P. Quis docebit me hoc?

M. Ego, cum DEO.

P. Quomodo?

M. Ducam te per omnia.

Ostendam tibi omnia.

Nominabo tibi omnia.

P. En, adsum; duc me in nomine DEI.

M. Ante omnia, debes discere simplices *Sonos* ex quibus *Sermo* humanus constat; quos *Animalia* sciunt *formare*, & tua *Lingua* scit *imitari*, & tua *Manus* potest *pingere*.

Postea ibimus *Mundum*, & spectabimus omnia.

Hic habes vivum et vocale Alphabetum.

Cornix cornicatur, à à The *Crow* crieth.	A a
Agnus balat, b è è è The *Lamb* blaiteth.	B b
Cicàda stridet, cì cì The *Grasshopper* chirpeth.	C c
Upupa dicit, du du The *Whooppoo* saith.	D d
Infans ejulat, è è è The *Infant* crieth.	E e
Ventus flat, fi fi The *Wind* bloweth.	F f
Anser gingrit, ga ga The *Goose* gagleth.	G g
Os halat, hà'h hà'h The *Mouth* breatheth out.	H h
Mus mintrit, ì ì ì The *Mouse* chirpeth.	I i
Anas tetrinnit, kha, kha The *Duck* quaketh.	K k
Lupus ululat, lu ulu The *Wolf* howleth.	L
[mum *Ursus* murmurat, mum- The *Bear* grumbleth.	M m

Felis clamat, nau nau The *Cat* crieth.	N n
Auriga clamat, ò ò ò The *Carter* crieth.	O o
Pullus pipit, pi pi The *Chicken* peepeth.	P p
Cúculus cuculat, kuk ku The *cuckow* singeth.	Q q
Canis ringitur, err The *dog* grinneth.	R r
Serpens sibilat, si The *Serpent* hisseth.	S s
Graculus clamat, tac tac The *Jay* crieth.	T t
Bubo ululat, ù ù The *Owl* hooteth.	U u
Lepus vagit, va The *Hare* squeaketh.	W w
Rana coaxat, coax The *Frog* croaketh.	X x
Asinus rudit, y y y The *Asse* brayeth.	Y y
Tabanus dicit, ds ds The *Breeze* or *Horse-flie* saith.	Z z

God   II.   Deus.

God is of himself from everlasting to everlasting.

A most perfect and a most blessed *Being*.

In his *Essence* Spiritual, and One.

In his *Personality*, Three.

In his *Will*, Holy, Just, Merciful and True.

In his *Power* very great.

In his *Goodness*, very good.

In his *Wisdom*, unmeasurable.

A *Light* inaccessible; and yet all in all.

Every where, and no where.

Deus est ex seipso, ab æterno in æternum.

Perfectissimum & beatissimum *Ens*.

Essentiâ Spiritualis & unus.

Hypostasi Trinus.

Voluntate, Sanctus, Justus, Clemens, Verax.

Potentiâ maximus.

Bonitate Optimus.

Sapientiâ, immensus.

Lux inaccessa;

& tamen omnia in omnibus.

Ubique & nullibi.

The chiefest *Good*, and the only and inexhausted Fountain of all good things.

Summum *Bonum*, et solus et inexhaustus Fons omnium Bonorum.

As the *Creator*, so the *Governour* and *Preserver* of all things, which we call the *World*.

Ut *Creator*, ita *Gubernator* et *Conservator* omnium rerum, quas vocamus *Mundum*.

The World.　　III.　　Mundus.

The *Heaven*, 1.
hath *Fire*, and *Stars*.
The *Clouds*, 2.
hang in the *Air*.
Birds, 3.
fly under the Clouds.
Fishes, 4.
swim in the *Water*.
The *Earth* hath *Hills*, 5.
Woods, 6. *Fields*, 7.
Beasts, 8. and *Men*, 9.

Cælum, 1.
habet *Ignem & Stellas*.
Nubes, 2.
pendent in *Aere*.
Aves, 3.
volant sub nubibus.
Pisces, 4.
natant in *Aqua*.
Terra habet *Montes*, 5.
Sylvas, 6. *Campos*, 7.
Animalia, 8. *Homines*, 9.

Thus the greatest *Bodies* of the World, the four *Elements*, are full of their own Inhabitants.	Ita maxima *Corpora* Mundi, quatuor *Elementa,* sunt plena Habitatoribus suis.

The Heaven.   IV.   Cœlum.

The Heaven, 1. is wheeled about, and encompasseth the *Earth*, 2. standing in the middle. The *Sun*, 3. wheresoever it is, shineth perpetually, howsoever dark *Clouds*, 4. may take it from us; and causeth by his *Rays*, 5. *Light*, and the Light, *Day*.	*Cœlum,* 1. rotatur, & ambit *Terram,* 2. stantem in medio. *Sol,* 3. ubi ubi est, fulget perpetuo, ut ut *densa Nubila,* 4. eripiant eum a nobis; facitque suis *Radiis,* 5. *Lucem,* Lux *Diem.*
On the other side, over against it, is *Darkness*, 6. and thence *Night*.	Ex opposito, sunt *Tenebræ,* 6. inde *Nox.*

In the Night	Nocte
shineth the *Moon*, 7.	splendet *Luna*, 7.
and the *Stars*, 8.	& *Stellæ*, 8.
glister and twinkle.	micant, scintillant.
In the Evening, 9.	Vesperi, 9.
is *Twilight:*	est *Crepusculum:*
In the *Morning*, 10.	Manè Aurora, 10.
the breaking, and	& Diluculum.
dawning of the Day.	

Fire.	V.	Ignis.

The *Fire* gloweth, burneth and consumeth to ashes.	*Ignis* ardet, urit, cremat.
A *spark* of it struck out of a *Flint* (or Firestone),2.	*Scintilla* ejus elisa e *Silice*, (Pyrite) 2.
by means of a *Steel*, 1.	Ope *Chalybis*, 1.
and taken by *Tynder* in a *Tynder-box*, 3.	et excepta a *Fomite* in *Suscitabulo*, 3.
lighteth a *Match*, 4.	accendit *Sulphuratum*, 4.
and after that a *Candle*, 5.	et inde *Candelam*, 5.

·or *stick*, 6.

and causeth a *flame*, 7.

·or *blaze*, 8.

which catcheth hold of

the Houses.

   Smoak, 9.

ascendeth therefrom,

which, sticking to the

Chimney, 10.

turneth into *Soot*.

   Of a *Fire-brand*,

(or burning stick)

is made a *Brand*, 11.

(or quenched stick).

   Of a *hot Coal*

(red hot piece

of a Fire-brand)

is made a *Coal*, 12.

(or a *dead Cinder*).

   That which remaineth,

is at last *Ashes*, 13.

and *Embers* (or hot *Ashes*).

vel *Lignum*, 6.

et excitat *Flammam*, 7.

vel *Incendium*, 8.

quod corripit

Æ dificia.

   Fumus, 9.

ascendit inde,

qui, adhærans

Camino, 10.

abit in *Fuliginem*.

   Ex *Torre*,

(ligno ardente,)

fit *Titio*, 11.

(lignum extinctum.)

   Ex *Pruna*,

(candente particulâ

Torris,)

fit *Carbo*, 12.

(*Particula mortua.*)

   Quod remanet,

tandem est *Cinis*, 13.

& *Favilla* (ardens *Cinis.*)

The Air.   VI.   Aër.

A cool *Air*, 1.
breatheth gently.
    The *Wind*, 2.
bloweth strongly.
    A *Storm*, 3.
throweth down Trees.
    A *Whirl-wind*, 4.
turneth it self in a round
compass.
    A Wind *under Ground*,5.
causeth an *Earthquake.*
    An Earthquake causeth
gapings of the Earth,
(and falls of Houses.) 6.

    Aura, 1.
spirat leniter.
    Ventus, 2.
flat valide.
    Procella, 3.
sternit Arbores.
    Turbo, 4.
agit se in gyrum.

    Ventus *subterraneus*, 5.
excitat *Terræ motum.*
    Terræ motus facit
Labes (& ruinas.) 6.

| The Water. | VII. | Aqua. |

The *Water* springeth out of a *Fountain*, 1.	*Aqua* scatet è *Fonte*, 1.
floweth downwards in a *Brook*, 2.	defluit in *Torrente*, 2.
runneth in a *Beck*, 3.	manat in *Rivo*, 3.
standeth in a *Pond*, 4.	stat in *Stagno*, 4.
glideth in a *Stream*, 5.	fluit in *Flumine*, 5.
is whirled about in a *Whirl-pit*, 6.	gyratur in *Vortice*, 6.
and causeth *Fens*, 7.	& facit *Paludes*, 7.
The *River* hath *Banks*, 8.	Flumen habet *Ripas*.
The *Sea* maketh *Shores*, 9.	*Mare* facit *Littora*, 9.
Bays, 10. *Capes*, 11.	*Sìnus*, 10. *Promontoria*, 11.
Islands, 12. *Almost Islands*, 13. *Necks of Land*, 14.	*Insulas*, 12. *Peninsulas*, 13. *Isthmos*, 14.
Straights, 15.	*Freta*, 15.
and hath in it *Rocks*, 16.	& habet *Scopulos*, 16.

The Clouds. VIII. Nubes.

A *Vapour*, 1. ascendeth from the *Water*.

From it a *Cloud*, 2. is made, and a *white Mist*, 3. near the Earth.

Rain, 4. and a small *Shower* distilleth out of a *Cloud*, drop by drop.

Which being frozen, is *Hail*, 5. half frozen is *Snow*, 6. being warm is *Mel-dew*.

In a rainy Cloud, set over against the Sun the *Rainbow*, 7. appeareth.

A *drop* falling into the water maketh a *Bubble*, 8. many *Bubbles* make froth, 9.

Frozen Water is called *Ice*, 10.

Dew congealed,

Vapor, 1. ascendit ex *Aquâ*.

Inde *Nubes*, 2. fit, et *Nebula*, 3. prope terram.

Pluvia, 4. et *Imber*, stillat e *Nube*, guttatim.

Quæ gelata, *Grando*, 5. semigelata, *Nix*, 6. calefacta, *Rubigo* est.

In nube pluviosâ, oppositâ soli *Iris*, 7. apparet.

Gutta incidens in aquam, facit *Bullam*, 8. multæ *Bullæ* faciunt spumam, 9.

Aqua congelata *Glacies*, 10.

Ros congelatus,

is called a *white Frost*.

Thunder is made of a brimstone-like *vapour*, which breaking out of a Cloud, with *Lightning*, 11. thundereth and striketh with lightning.

dicitur *Pruina*.

Tonitru fit ex *Vapore* sulphureo, quod erumpens è Nube cum *Fulgure*, 11. tonat & fulminat.

The Earth.   IX.   Terra.

In the *Earth* are high *Mountains*, 1.
Deep *Vallies*, 2.
Hills rising, 3.
Hollow Caves, 4.
Plain *Fields*, 5.
Shady *Wood*s, 6.

In *Terra* sunt
Alti *Montes*, 1.
Profundæ *valles*, 2.
Elevati Colles, 3.
cavæ Speluncæ, 4.
Plani *campi*, 5.
Opacæ Sylvæ, 6.

The Fruits of the Earth.   X.   Terræ Fœtus.

A *meadow*, 1. yieldeth *grass* with *Flowers* and *Herbs*, which being cut down, are made *Hay*, 2.

A *Field*, 3. yieldeth *Corn*, and *Pot-herbs*, 4.

Mushrooms, 5.
Straw-berries, 6.
Myrtle-trees, &c.
come up in Woods.

Metals, Stones, and *Minerals*
grow *under the earth*.

Pratum, 1. fert *Gramina*, cum *Floribus* & *Herbis* quæ defecta fiunt *Fœnum*, 2.

Arvum, 3. fert *Fruges*, & *Olera*, 4.

Fungi, 5.
Fraga, 6.
Myrtilli, &c.
Proveniunt in Sylvis.

Metalla, Lapides, Mineralia,
nascuntur sub terra.

Metals.   XI.   Metalla.

Lead, 1.	*Plumbum,* 1.
is soft, and heavy.	est molle & grave.
Iron, 2. is hard,	*Ferrum,* 2. est durum,
and *Steel,* 3. harder.	& *Calybs,* 3. durior.
They make *Tankards*	Faciunt *Cantharos,* 4.
(or *Cans*), 4. of *Tin.*	e *Stanno.*
Kettles, 5. of *Copper,*	*Ahena,* 5, e *Cupro,*
Candlesticks, 6. of *Latin,*	*Candelabra,* 6. ex *Orichalco,*
Dollers, 7. of *Silver,*	*Thaleros,* 7. ex *Argento,*
Ducats and *Crown-pieces,* 8.	*Scutatos* et *Coronatos,* 8.
Quick-silver is always li-	Ex, *Auro.*
quid, and eateth thorow	*Argentum Vivum,* semper
Metals of Gold.	liquet, & corrodit *Metalla.*

Stones.　　　　　XII.　　　　　Lapides.

Sand, 1. and *Gravel*, 2.	*Arena*, 1. & *Sabulum*, 2.
is *Stone* broken into bits.	est *Lapis* comminutus.
A *great Stone*, 3.	*Saxum*, 3.
is a piece of	est pars
a *Rock* (or Crag) 4.	*Petræ* (Cautis) 4.
A *Whetstone*, 5.	*Cos*, 5.
a *Flint*, 6. a *Marble*, 7. &c.	*Silex*, 6. *Marmor*, 7. &c.
are ordinary Stones.	sunt obscuri Lapides.
A *Load-stone*, 8.	*Magnes*, 8.
draweth Iron to it.	adtrahit ferrum.
Jewels, 9.	*Gemmæ*, 9.
are clear Stones, as	sunt pellucidi Lapilli, ut
The *Diamond* white,	*Adamas* candidus,
The *Ruby* red,	*Rubinus* rubeus,
The *Sapphire* blue,	*Sapphirus* cæruleus,
The *Emerald* green,	*Smaragdus* viridis,
The *Jacinth* yellow, &c.	*Hyacynthus* luteus, &c.
And they glister	et micant
being cut into corners.	angulati.
Pearls and *Unions*, 10.	*Margaritæ* & *Uniones*, 10.
grow in Shell-fish.	crescunt in Conchis.

Corals, 11. in a Sea-shrub.	*Corallia*, 11. in Marinâ arbusculâ.
Amber, 12. is gathered from the Sea.	*Succinum*, 12. colligitur è mari.
Glass, 13. is like *Chrystal*.	*Vitrum*, 13. simile est *Chrystallo*.

Tree.	XIII.	Arbor.

A *Plant*, 1. groweth from a *Seed*.	*Planta*, 1. procrescit e *Semine*.
A plant waxeth to a *Shoot*, 2.	Planta abit in *Fruticem*, 2.
A *Shoot* to a *Tree*, 3.	*Frutex* in *Arborem*, 3.
The *Root*, 4.	*Radix*, 4.
beareth up the Tree.	Sustentat arborem.
The *Body* or *Stem*, 5. riseth from the Root.	*Stirps* (*Stemma*) 5. Surgit e radice.
The *Stem* divideth it self into *Boughs*, 6. and green *Branches*, 7. made of *Leaves*, 8.	*Stirps* se dividit in *Ramos*, 6. & *Frondes*, 7. factas e *Foliis*, 8.

D

The *top*, 9.	*Cacumen*, 9.
is in the height.	est in summo.
The *Stock*, 10.	*Truncus*, 10.
is close to the roots.	adhærat radicibus.
A *Log*, 11.	*Caudex*, 11.
is the body fell'd down	est Stipes dejectus,
without Boughs; having	sine ramis; habens *Cor-*
Bark and *Rind*, 12.	*ticem* & *Librum*, 12.
Pith and *Heart*, 13.	*pulpam* & *medullam*, 13.
Bird-lime, 14.	*Viscum*, 14.
groweth upon the boughs,	adnascitur *ramis*,
which also sweat	qui etiam sudant,
Gumm,	*Gummi*,
Rosin,	*Resinam*,
Pitch, &c.	*Picem*, &c.

Fruits of Trees.	XIV.	Fructus Arborum.

Fruits that have no	*Poma*
shells are pull'd from	decerpuntur,
fruit-bearing trees.	a fructiferis arboribus.
The *Apple*, 1. is round.	*Malum*, 1. est rotundum.

The *Pear*, 2. and *Fig*, 3. | *Pyrum*, 2. & *Ficus*, 3.
are something long. | sunt oblonga.
 The *Cherry*, 4. | *Cerasum*, 4.
hangeth by a long start. | pendet longo *Pediolo*.
 The *Plumb*, 5. | *Prunum*, 5.
and *Peach*, 6. | & *Persicum*, 6.
by a shorter. | breviori.
 The *Mulberry*, 7. | *Morum*, 7.
by a very short one. | brevissimo.
 The *Wall-nut*, 8. | *Nux Juglans*, 8.
the *Hazel-nut*, 9. | *Avellana*, 9.
and *Chest-nut*, 10. | & *Castanea*, 10.
are wrapped in a *husk* | involuta sunt *Cortici*
and a *Shell*. | & *Putamini*.
 Barren trees are 11. | Steriles arbores sunt 11.
The *Firr*, the *Alder*, | *Abies, Alnus,*
The *Birch*, the *Cypress*, | *Betula, Cupressus,*
The *Beech*, the *Ash*, | *Fagus, Fraxinus,*
The *Sallow*, the *Linden-tree*, | *Salix, Tilia*, &c.
&c., but most of them af- | sed pleræque umbriferæ.
fording shade. |
 But the *Juniper*, 12. | At *Juniperus*, 12.
and *Bay-tree*, 13. yield | & *Laurus*, 13. ferunt
Berries. | *Baccas*.
 The *Pine*, 14. *Pine-apples*. | *Pinus*, 14. *Strobilos*.
 The *Oak*, 15. | *Quercus*, 15.
Acorns and *Galls*. | *Glandes* & *Gallas*.

Flowers.   XV.   Flores..

Amongst the Flowers the most noted,

In the beginning of the Spring are the
Violet, 1. the *Crow-toes*, 2. the *Daffodil*, 3.

Then the *Lillies*, 4. white and yellow and blew, 5.
and the *Rose*, 6. and the *Clove-gilliflowers*, 7. &c.

Of these *Garlands*, 8. and *Nosegays*, 9. are tyed round with twigs.

There are added also *sweet herbs*, 10.
as *Marjoram, Flower gentle, Rue, Lavender, Rosemary*.

Inter flores notissimi,

Primo vere,

Viola, 1. *Hyacinthus*, 2. *Narcissus*, 3.

Tum *Lilia*, 4. alba & lutea, & cœrulea, 5.
tandem *Rosa*, 6. & *Caryophillum*, 7. &c.

Ex his *Serta*, 8. & *Serviæ*, 9. vientur.

Adduntur etiam *Herbæ odoratæ*, 10.
ut *Amaracus, Amaranthus, Ruta, Lavendula, Rosmarinus*, (Libanotis).

Hysop, Spike,	*Hypossus, Nard,*
Basil, Sage,	*Ocymum, Salvia,*
Mints, &c.	*Menta,* &c.
Amongst Field-flowers,	Inter Campestres
11. the most noted are	Flores, 11. notissimi sunt
the *May-lillie,*	*Lilium Convallium,*
Germander, the *Blew-Bottle,*	*Chamædrys, Cyanus,*
Chamomel, &c.	*Chamæmelum,* &c.
And amongst Herbs,	Et Herbæ,
Trefoil.	*Cytisus* (Trifolium)
Wormwood, Sorrel,	*Absinthium, Acetosa,*
the *Nettle,* &c.	*Urtica,* &c.
The *Tulip,* 12.	*Tulipa,* 12.
is the grace of flowers,	est decus Florum,
but affording no smell.	sed expers odoris.

Potherbs.	XVI.	Olera.

Pot-herbs	*Olera*
grow in Gardens,	nascuntur in hortis,
as *Lettice,* 1.	ut *Lactuca,* 1.
Colewort, 2.	*Brassica,* 2.
Onions, 3.	*Cepa,* 3.

Garlick, 4. Gourd, 5.	Allium, 4. Cucurbita, 5.
The Parsnep, 6.	Siser, 6.
The Turnep, 7.	Rapa, 7.
The Radish, 8.	Raphanus minor, 8.
Horse-radish, 9.	Raphanus major, 9.
Parsly, 10.	Petroselinum, 10.
Cucumbers, 11.	Cucumeres, 11.
and Pompions, 12.	Pepones, 12.

Corn.   XVII.   Fruges.

Some *Corn* grows upon a *straw*, parted by *knots*, as *Wheat*, 1. *Rie*, 2, *Barley*, 3. in which the *Ear* hath *awnes*, or else it is without awnes, and it nourisheth the *Corn* in the *Husk*.

Some instead of an ear, have a *rizom* (or plume) containing the corn by bunches, as *Oats*, 4. *Millet*, 5. *Turkey-wheat*, 6.

Frumenta quædam crescunt super *culmum*, distinctum *geniculis*, ut, *Triticum*, 1. *Siligo*, 2. *Hordeum*, 3. in quibus *Spica* habet *Aristas*, aut est mutica, fovetque *grana* in *gluma*.

Quædam pro Spica, habent *Paniculam*, continentem grana fasciatim, ut, *Avena*, 4. *Milium*, 5. *Frumentum Saracenicum*, 6.

Pulse have *Cods*,	*Legumina* habent *Siliquas*,
which enclose the corns	quæ includunt grana
in two *Shales*,	*valvulis*,
as *Pease*, 7.	ut, *Pisum*, 7.
Beans, 8. *Vetches*, 9. and	*Fabæ*, 8. *Vicia*, 9.
those that are less than	& minores his
these *Lentils* and *Urles* (or	*Lentes* & *Cicera*.
Tares).	

Shrubs.   XVIII.   Frutices.

A plant being greater,	Planta major
and harder than an herb,	& durior herba,
is called a *Shrub:*	dicitur *Frutex :*
such as are	ut sunt
In Banks and Ponds,	In ripis & stagnis,
the *Rush*, 1.	*Juncus*, 1.
the *Bulrush*, 2.	*Scirpus*, 2.
or Cane without knots	[Canna] *enodis*
bearing *Cats-tails*,	ferens *Typhos*,
and the *Reed*, 3.	& *Arundo*, 3.
which is knotty and hol-	nodosa et cava
low within.	intus.
Elsewhere, 4.	Alibi, 4.

the *Rose*,	*Rosa*,
the *Bastard-Corinths*,	*Ribes*,
the *Elder*, the *Juniper*.	*Sambucus*, *Juniperus*,
Also the *Vine*, 5. which	Item *Vitis*, 5.
putteth forth *branches*, 6.	quæ emittit *Palmites*, 6.
and these *tendrels*, 7.	et hi *Capreolos*, 7.
Vine-leaves, 8.	*Pampinos*. 8.
and Bunches of grapes, 9.	et *Racemos*, 9.
on the stock whereof	quorum Scapo
hang *Grapes*,	pendent *Uvæ*,
which contain *Grape-stones*.	continentes *Acinos*.

XIX.

Living-Creatures: and First, Birds.

Animalia: & primum, Aves.

A *living Creature* liveth,	*Animal* vivit,
perceiveth, moveth it self;	sentit, movet se;
is born, dieth,	nascitur, moritur,
is nourished,	nutritur,
and groweth: standeth,	& crescit; stat,
or sitteth, or lieth,	aut sedet, aut cubat,
or goeth.	aut graditur.

A *Bird*, (*Fisher*, 1. here the King's making her nest in the Sea.)	*Avis*, (hic *Halcyon*, 1. in mari nidulans.)
is covered with *Feathers*,2.	tegitur *Plumis*, 2.
flyeth with *Wings*, 3.	volat *Pennis*, 3.
hath two *Pinions*, 4.	habet duas *Alas*, 4.
as many *Feet*, 5.	totidem *Pedes*, 5.
a *Tail*, 6.	*Caudam*, 6.
and a *Bill*, 7.	& *Rostrum*, 7.
The *Shee*, 8. layeth Eggs, 10. in a nest, 9.	*Fœmella*, 8. *ponit* Ova, 10. in nido, 9.
and sitting upon them,	et incubans iis,
hatcheth *young ones*, 11.	excludit *Pullos*, 11.
An *Egg* is cover'd with a *Shell*, 12.	*Ovum* tegitur *testa*, 12.
under which is the *White*, 13.	sub qua est *Albumen*, 13.
in this the *Yolk*, 14.	in hoc *Vitellus*, 14.

Tame Fowls.	XX.	Aves Domesticæ.

The *Cock*, 1. (which croweth in the Morning.)	*Gallus*, 1. (qui cantat mane.)

English	Latin
hath a *Comb*, 2.	habet *Cristam*, 2.
and *Spurs*, 3.	& *Calcaria*, 3.
being gelded, he is called	castratus dicitur
a *Capon*, and is crammed	*Capo* & saginatur
in a *Coop*, 4.	in *Ornithotrophico*, 4.
A *Hen*, 5.	*Gallina*, 5.
scrapeth the *Dunghil*,	ruspatur *fimetum*,
and picketh up Corns:	& colligit grana:
as also the *Pigeons*, 6.	sicut & *Columbæ*, 6,
(which are brought up in	(quæ educantur in *Colum-*
a *Pigeon-house*, 7.)	*bario*, 7.)
and the *Turkey-cock*, 8.	& *Gallopavus*, 8.
with his *Turkey-hen*, 9.	cum sua *Meleagride*, 9.
The gay *Peacock*, 10.	Formosus *Pavo*, 10.
prideth in his Feathers.	superbit pennis.
The *Stork*, 11.	*Ciconia*, 11.
buildeth her nest	nidificat
on the top of the House,	in tecto.
The *Swallow*, 12.	*Hirundo*, 12.
the *Sparrow*, 13.	*Passer*, 13.
the *Mag-pie*, 14.	*Pica*, 14.
the *Jackdaw*, 15.	*Monedula*, 15.
and the *Bat*, 16.	& *Vespertilio*, 16.
(or Flettermouse)	(Mus alatus)
use to flie about Houses.	volitant circa Domus.

Singing-Birds.   XXI.   Oscines.

The *Nightingal*, 1. sing-eth the sweetlyest of all.	*Luscinia* (*Philomela*), 1. cantat suavissime omnium.

The *Nightingal*, 1. singeth the sweetlyest of all.
   The *Lark*, 2. singeth
as she flyeth in the Air.
   The *Quail*, 3.
sitting on the ground;
others on the boughs of
trees, 4. as the *Canary-bird*,
the *Chaffinch*,
the *Goldfinch*,
the *Siskin*,
the *Linnet*,
the little *Titmouse*,
the *Wood-wall*,
the *Robin-red-breast*,
the *Hedge-sparrow*, &c.
   The party colour'd *Par-
ret*, 5. the *Black-bird*, 6.
the *Stare*, 7.
with the *Mag-pie*
and the *Jay*, learn

Luscinia (*Philomela*), 1.
cantat suavissime omnium.
   Alauda, 2. cantillat
volitans in aere;
   Coturnix, 3.
sedens humi;
   Cæteræ, in ramis arbor-
um, 4. ut *Luteola* peregrina.
Fringilla,
Carduelis,
Acanthis,
Linaria,
parvus *Parus*,
Galgulus,
Rubecula,
Curruca, &c.
   Discolor *Psittacus*, 5.
Merula, 6.
Sturnus, 7.
cum *Pica*,
& *Monedula*, discunt

to frame men's words.

  A great many are wont
to be shut in *Cages*, 8.

humanas voces formare

  Pleræque solent
includi *Caveis*, 8.

XXII.

Birds that haunt the Fields and Woods.

Aves Campestres & Sylvestres.

  The *Ostrich*, 1.
is the greatest Bird.
  The *Wren*, 2.
is the least.
  The *Owl*, 3.
is the most despicable.
  The *Whoopoo*, 4.
is the most nasty,
for it eateth dung.
  The *Bird of Paradise*, 5.
is very rare.
  The *Pheasant*, 6.
the *Bustard*, 7.

  Struthio, 1.
ales est maximus.
  Regulus, 2. (Trochilus)
minimus.
  Noctua, 3.
despicatissimus.
  Upupa, 4.
sordidssimus,
vescitur enim stercoribus.
  Manucodiata, 5.
rarissimus.
  Phasianus, 6.
Tarda (Otis), 7.

the deaf wild *Peacock*, 8.	surdus, *Tetrao*, 8.
the *Moor-hen*, 9.	*Attagen*, 9.
the *Partrige*, 10.	*Perdix*, 10.
the *Woodcock*, 11.	*Gallinago* (Rusticola), 11.
and the *Thrush*, 12.	& *Turdus*, 12,
are counted Dainties.	habentur in deliciis.
Among the rest,	Inter reliquas,
the best are,	potissimæ sunt,
the watchful *Crane*, 13.	*Grus*, 13. pervigil.
the mournful *Turtle*, 14.	*Turtur*, 14. gemens.
the *Cuckow*, 15.	*Cuculus*, 15.
the *Stock-dove*,	*Palumbes*,
the *Speight*, the *Jay*,	*Picus*, *Garrulus*,
the *Crow*, &c., 16.	*Cornix*, &c., 16.

Ravenous Birds.	XXIII.	Aves Rapaces.

The *Eagle*, 1.	*Aquila*, 1.
the King of Birds	Rex Avium,
looketh upon the Sun,	intuetur Solem.
The *Vulture*, 2.	*Vultur*, 2.
and the *Raven*, 3.	& *Corvus*, 3.

feed upon *Carrion*. | pascuntur *morticinis*, [cadaveribus.]

The *Kite*, 4. pursueth Chickens. | *Milvus*, 4. insectatur pullos gallinaceos.

The *Falcon*, 5. the *Hobbie*, 6. and the *Hawk*, 7. catch at little Birds. | *Falco*, 5, *Nisus*, 6. & *Accipiter*, 7. captant aviculas.

The *Gerfalcon*, 8. catcheth Pigeons and greater Birds. | *Astur*, 8. captat columbas & aves majores.

Water-Fowl.　　　XXIV.　　　Aves Aquaticæ.

The white *Swan*, 1. the *Goose*, 2. and the *Duck*, 3. swim up and down. | *Oler*, 1. candidus, *Anser*, 2. & *Anas*, 3. natant.

The *Cormorant*, 4, diveth. | *Mergus*, 4. se mergit.

And to these the water-hen, and the *Pelican*, &c., 10. | Adde his Fulicam, *Pelecanum*, &c., 10.

The *Osprey*, 5.	*Halicætus*, 5.
and the *Sea-mew*, 6.	& *Gavia*, 6.
flying downwards	devolantes,
use to catch Fish,	captant pisces,
but the *Heron*, 7.	sed *Ardea*, 7.
standing on the Banks.	stans in ripis.
The *Bittern*, 8, putteth	*Butio*, 8.
his Bill in the water, and	inferit rostrum aquæ,
belloweth like an Ox.	& mugit ut bos.
The *Water-wagtail*, 9.	*Motacilla*, 9.
waggeth the tail.	motat caudam.

Flying Vermin.   XXV.   Insecta volantia.

The *Bee*, 1. maketh honey	*Apis*, 1. facit mel
which the *Drone*, 2. devour-	quod *Fucus*, 2. depascit
eth. The *Wasp*, 3.	*Vespa*, 3.
and the *Hornet*, 4.	& *Crabro*, 4.
molest with a sting;	infestant oculeo ;
and the *Gad-Bee*	& *Oestrum*
(or Breese), 5.	(Asilus), 5.
especially *Cattel*;	imprimis *pecus*.

but the *Fly*, 6.
and the *Gnat*, 7. us.
   The *Cricket*, 8. singeth.
   The *Butterfly*, 9. is a
winged *Caterpillar*.
   The *Beetle*, 10. covereth
her wings with *Cases.*
   The *Glow-worm*, 11.
shineth by night.

autem *Musca*, 6.
& *Culex*, 7. nos.
   Gryllus, 8. *cantillat.*
   Papillio, 9. est
alata *Eruca.*
   Scarabæus, 10. tegit
alas *vaginis.*
   Cicindela [Lampyris], 11.
nitet noctu.

XXVI.

Four-Footed Beasts: and First those about the House.

Quadrupeda : & primum Domestica.

   The *Dog*, 1.
with the *Whelp*, 2.
is keeper of the House.
   The *Cat*, 3.

   Canis, 1.
cum *Catello*, 2.
est custos Domûs.
   Felis (Catus) 3.

riddeth the House	purgat domum
of *Mice*, 4.	à *Muribus*, 4.
which also a	quod etiam
Mouse-trap, 5. doth.	*Muscipula*, 5. facit.
A *Squirrel*, 6.	*Sciurus*, 6.
The *Ape*, 7.	*Simia*, 7.
and the *Monkey*, 8.	& *Cercopithecus*, 8.
are kept at home	habentur domi
for delight.	delectamento.
The *Dormouse*, 9. and	*Glis*, 9. &
other greater Mice, 10.	cæteri Mures majores, 10.
as, the *Weesel*, the *Marten*,	ut, *Mustela*, *Martes*,
and the *Ferret*,	*Viverra*,
trouble the House,	infestant domum.

Herd-Cattle.	XXVII.	Pecora.

The *Bull*, 1. the *Cow*, 2.	*Taurus*, 1. *Vacca*, 2.
and the *Calf*, 3.	& *Vitulus*, 3.
are covered with hair.	teguntur pilis.
The *Ram*, the *Weather*, 4.	*Aries*, *Vervex*, 4.
the *Ewe*, 5. and the *Lamb*, 6.	*Ovis*, 5. cum *Agno*, 6.
bear wool.	gestant lanam.

E

The *He-goat*, the *Gelt-goat*, 7.	*Hircus, Caper*, 7.
with the *She-goat*, 8.	cum *Capra*, 8.
and *Kid*, 9. have	& *Hœdo*, 9. habent.
shag-hair and *beards*.	*Villos* & *aruncos*.
The *Hog*, the *Sow*, 10.	*Porcus, Scrofa*, 10.
and the *Pigs*, 11.	cum *Porcellis*, 11.
have *bristles*,	habent *Setas*,
but not *horns*;	at non *Cornua* ;
but also *cloven feet*	sed etiam *Ungulas bisulcas*
as those others (have.)	ut illa.

Labouring-Beasts.	XXVIII.	Jumenta.

The *Ass*, 1.	*Asinus*, 1.
and the *Mule*, 2.	& *Mulus*, 2.
carry burthens.	gestant Onera.
The *Horse*, 3.	*Equus*, 3.
(which a *Mane*, 4. graceth) carryeth us.	(quam *Juba*, 4. ornat) gestat nos ipsos.
The *Camel*, 5.	*Camelus*, 5.
carryeth the Merchant with his Ware.	gestat Mercatorem cum mercibus suis.

The *Elephant*, 6.	*Elephas*, (Barrus) 6.
draweth his meat to him	attrahit pabulum
with his *Trunk*, 7.	*Proboscide*, 7.
He hath two *Teeth*, 8.	Habet duos *dentes*, 8.
standing out,	prominentes,
and is able to carry	& potest portare
full thirty men.	etiam triginta viros.

Wild-Cattle.	XXIX.	Feræ Pecudes.

The *Buff*, 1.	*Urus*, 1.
and the *Buffal*, 2.	& *Bubalus*, 2.
are wild Bulls.	sunt feri Boves.
The *Elke*, 3.	*Alces*, 3.
being bigger than an	major equo
Horse (whose back is im-	(cujus tergus est impene-
penetrable) hath knaggy	trabilis) habet ramosa cor-
horns as also the *Hart*, 4.	nua; ut & *Cervus*, 4.
but the *Roe*, 5. and	Sed *Caprea*, 5.
the *Hind-calf*, almost none.	cum *Hinnulo*, ferè nulla.
The *Stone-back*, 6.	*Capricornus*, 6.
huge great ones.	prægrandia;
The *Wild-goat*, 7.	*Rupicapra*, 7.
hath very little ones,	minuta,
by which she hangeth	quibus suspendit
her self on a Rock.	se ad rupem.

The *Unicorn*, 8. | *Monoceros*, 8.
hath but one, | habet unum,
but that a precious one. | sed pretiosum.
The *Boar*, 9. assail- | *Aper*, 9.
eth one with his tushes. | grassatur dentibus.
The *Hare*, 10. is fearful. | *Lepus*, 10. pavet.
The *Cony*, 11. | *Cuniculus*, 11.
diggeth the Earth. | perfodit *terram* ;
As also the *Mole*, 12. | Ut & *Talpa*, 12.
which maketh hillocks. | quæ facit grumos.

Wild-Beasts.   XXX.   Feræ Besitæ.

Wild Beasts | *Bestiæ*
have sharp paws, and | habent acutos ungues, &
teeth, and are flesh eaters. | dentes,suntque carnivoræ,
As the *Lyon*, 1. | Ut *Leo*, 1.
the King of four-footed | Rex quadrupedum,
Beasts, having a mane; | jubatus;
with the *Lioness*. | cum *Leænâ*.
The spotted *Panther*, 2. | Maculosus, *Pardo* (Pan--thera) 2.

The *Tyger*, 3.	*Tygris*, 3.
the cruellest of all.	immanissima omnium.
The Shaggy *Bear*, 4.	Villosus *Ursus*, 4.
The ravenous *Wolf*, 5.	Rapax *Lupus*, 5.
The quick sighted *Ounce*, 6.	*Lynx*, 6. visu pollens,
The tayled *fox*, 7.	Caudata *Vulpes*, 7.
the craftiest of all.	astutissima *omnium*.
The *Hedge-hog*, 8.	*Erinaceus*, 8.
is prickly.	est aculeatus.
The *Badger*, 9.	*Melis*, 9.
delighteth in holes.	gaudet latebris.

XXXI.
Serpents and Creeping things.

Serpentes & Reptilia.

Snakes creep	*Angues* repunt
by winding themselves;	sinuando se;
The *Adder*, 1.	*Coluber*, 1.
in the wood;	in Sylvâ;
The *Water-snake*, 2.	*Natrix*, (hydra) 2.
in the water;	in Aquâ;
The *Viper*, 3.	*Vipera*, 3.
amongst great stones.	in saxis;

The *Asp*, 4. in the fields. | *Aspis*, 4, in campis.
The *Boa*,(or Mild-snake) | *Boa*, 5.
5. in Houses. | in Domibus.
The *Slow-worm*, 6. | *Cæcilia*, 6.
is blind. | est cœca.
The *Lizzard*, 7. | *Lacerta*, 7.
and the *Salamander*, 8. | *Salamandra*, 8.
(that liveth long in fire) | (in igne vivax,) habent
have feet. | pedes.

The *Dragon*, 9. | *Draco*, 9.
a winged Serpent, | *Serpens alatus*,
killeth with his Breath. | necat halitu.
The *Basilisk*, 10. | *Basiliscus*, 10.
with his Eyes; | Oculis;
And the *Scorpion*, 11. | *Scorpio*, 11.
with his poysonous tail. | venenatâ caudâ.

Crawling-Vermin.   XXXII.   Insecta repentia.

Worms gnaw *things*. | *Vermes*, rodunt *res*.

The *Earth-worm*, 1.	*Lumbricus*, 1.
the Earth.	terram.
The *Caterpillar*, 2.	*Eruca*, 2.
the Plant.	plantam.
The *Grashopper*, 3.	*Cicada*, 3.
the Fruits.	Fruges.
The *Mite*, 4. the Corn.	*Circulio*, 4. Frumenta.
The *Timber-worm*, 5.	*Teredo*, (cossis) 5.
Wood.	Ligna.
The *Moth*, 6. a garment.	*Tinea*, 6. vestem.
The *Book-worm*, 7.	*Blatta*, 7.
a Book.	Librum.
Maggots, 8.	*Termites*, 8.
Flesh and Cheese.	carnem & caseum.
Hand-worms, the Hair.	*Acari*, Capillum.
The skipping *Flea*, 9.	Saltans *Pulex*, 9.
the *Lowse*, 10.	*Pediculus*, 10.
and the stinking	fœtans *Cimex*, 11.
Wall-louse, 11. bite us.	mordent nos.
The *Tike*, 12.	*Ricinus*, 12.
is a blood-sucker.	sanguisugus est.
The *Silk-worm*, 13.	*Bombyx*, 13.
maketh silk.	facit sericum.
The *Pismire*, 14.	*Formica*, 14.
is painful.	est laboriosa.
The *Spider*, 15.	*Aranea*, 15.
weaveth a Cobweb,	texit Araneum,
nets for flies.	retia muscis.
The *Snail*, 16. carri-	*Cochlea*, 16.
eth about her Snail-horn.	circumfert testam.

XXXIII.

Creatures that live as well by Water as by Land.

Amphibia.

Creatures that live by land and by water, are	Viventia in terrâ & aquâ, sunt
The *Crocodile*, 1.	*Crocodilus*, 1.
a cruel and preying Beast of the River *Nilus ;*	immanis & prædatrix bestia *Nili* fluminis ;
The *Castor* or *Beaver*, 2.	*Castor*, (Fiber) 2.
having feet like a Goose, and a scaly tail to swim.	habens pedes anserinos & squameam Caudam ad natandum.
The *Otter*, 3.	*Lutra*, 3.
The croaking *Frog*, 4. with the *Toad*.	& coaxans *Rana*, 4. cum *Bufone*.
The *Tortoise*, 5.	*Testudo*, 5.
covered above and beneath with shells, as with a target.	Operta & infra, testis, ceu scuto.

XXXIV.
River Fish and Pond Fish.

Pisces Fluviatiles & Lacustres.

A *Fish* hath *Fins*, 1.
with which it swimmeth,
and *Gills*, 2.
by which it taketh breath,
and *Prickles*
instead of bones: besides
the *Male* hath a *Milt*,
and the *Female* a *Row*.
  Some have *Scales*.
as the *Carp*, 3.
and the *Luce* or *Pike*, 4.
  Some are sleek
as the *Eel*, 5.
and the *Lamprey*, 6.
  The *Sturgeon*, 7.
having a sharp snout,
groweth beyond the
length of a Man.
  The *Sheath-fish*, 8.

Piscis habet *Pinnas*, 1.
quibus natat;
& *Branchias*, 2.
quibus respirat;
& *Spinas*
loco ossium : præterea,
Mas Lactes,
Fœmina Ova.
  Quidam habent *Squamas*,
ut *Carpio*, 3.
Lucius, (Lupus) 4.
  Alii sunt glabri,
ut, *Anguilla*, 5.
Mustela, 6.
  Accipenser (Sturio), 7.
mucronatus, crescit
ultra longitudinem viri.

  Silurus, 8.

having wide Cheeks,
is bigger than he :
But the greatest,
is the *Huson*, 9.
Minews, 10.
swimming by shoals,
are the least.
Others of this sort are
the *Perch*, the *Bley*,
the *Barbel*,
the *Esch*, the *Trout*,
the *Gudgeon*, and *Trench*,11.
The *Crab-fish*, 12. is covered with a shell, and it
hath *Claws*, and crawleth
forwards and backwards.
The *Horse-leech*, 13.
sucketh blood.

bucculentus,
major illo est :
Sed maximus
Antaseus (Huso,) 9.
Apuæ, 10.
natantes gregatim,
sunt minutissimæ.
Alii hujus generis sunt
Perca, Alburnus,
Mullus, (Barbus)
Thymallus, Trutta,
Gobius, Tinca, 11.
Cancer, 12.
tegitur *crusta*,
habetque *chelas*, & gradi-
tur porro & retrò.
Hirudo, 13.
sugit sanguinem.

XXXV.

Sea-fish, and Shell-fish.　　Marini pisces & Conchæ.

The *Whale*, 1. is the
greatest of the Sea-fish.

Balæna, (Cetus) 1. max-
imus Piscium marinorum.

The *Dolphin*, 2.	*Delphinus*, 2.
the swiftest.	velocissimus.
The *Scate*, 3.	*Raia*, 3.
the most monstrous.	monstrossimus.
Others are the *Lamprel*,4	Alii sunt *Murænula*, 4.
the *Salmon*, or the *Lax*, 5.	*Salmo*, (Esox) 5.
There are also fish that	Danturetiam volatiles,6.
flie, 6. Add *Herrings*, 7.	Adde *Haleces*, 7.
which are brought pickled,	qui salsi,
and *Place*, 8. and *Cods*, 9.	& *Passeres*,8. cum *Asellis*,9.
which are brought dry;	qui adferuntur arefacti ;
and the Sea monsters,	& monstra marina,
the *Seal*. 10.	*Phocam*, 10.
and the *Sea-horse*, &c.	*Hippopotamum*, &c.
Shell-fish,11. have Shells.	*Concha*, 11. habet testas,
The *Oyster*, 12.	*Ostrea*, 12.
affordeth sweet meat.	dat sapidam carnem.
The *Purple-fish*, 13.	*Murex*, 13.
purple;	purpuram;
The others, Pearls, 14.	*Alii*, 14. Margaritas.

Man.	XXXVI.	Homo.

Adam, 1. the first Man. | *Adamus*, 1. primus Homo,

was made by God after
his own Image the sixth
day of the Creation, of a
lump of Earth.

And *Eve*, 2.
the first Woman, was made
of the Rib of the Man.

These, being tempted
by the *Devil* under the
shape of a *Serpent*, 3.
when they had eaten of the
fruit of the *forbidden Tree*,
4. were condemned, 5.
to misery and death,
with all their posterity,
and cast out of *Paradise*, 6.

formatus est a Deo
ad Imaginem suam
sextâ die Creationis,
e Gleba Terræ.

Et *Eva*, 2.
prima mulier,
formata est e costâ viri.

Hi, seducti
abolo sub specie
Serpentis, 3.
cum comederent
de fructu *vetitæ arboris*, 4.
damnati sunt, 5.
ad miseriam & mortem,
cum omni posteritate sua,
& ejecti e *Paradiso* 6.

XXXVII.
The Seven Ages of Man.

Septem Ætates Hominis.

A *Man* is first an *Infant*, 1. | *Homo* est primum *Infans*, 1.

then a *Boy*, 2.	deinde *Puer*, 2.
then a *Youth*, 3.	tum *Adolescens*, 3.
then a *Young-man*, 4.	inde *Juvenis*, 4.
then a *Man*, 5.	posteà *Vir*, 5.
after that an *Elderly-man*,6.	dehinc *Senex*, 6.
and at last, a *decrepid old man*, 7.	tandem *Silicernium*, 7.

So also in the other *Sex*, there are, a *Girl*, 8.	Sic etiam in altero *Sexu*, sunt, *Pupa*, 8.
A *Damosel*, 9. a *Maid*, 10.	*Puella*, 9. *Virgo*, 10.
A *Woman*, 11.	*Mulier*, 11.
an *elderly Woman*, 12. and	*Vetula*, 12.
a *decrepid old Woman*, 13.	*Anus decrepita*, 13.

XXXVIII.
The Outward Parts of a Man.

Membra Hominis Externa.

The *Head*, 1. is above,	*Caput*, 1. est supra,
the *Feet*, 20. below.	infra *Pedes*, 20.

the fore part of the Neck (which ends at the *Arm-holes*, 2.) is the *Throat*, 3. the hinder part, the *Crag*, 4.

The *Breast*, 5, is before; the *back*, 6, behind; Women have in it two *Dugs*, 7. with *Nipples*,

Under the Breast is the *Belly*, 9. in the middle of it the *Navel*, 10. underneath the *Groyn*, 11. and the *privities*.

The *Shoulder-blades*, 12. are behind the back, on which the *Shoulders* depend, 13. on these the *Arms*, 14. with the *Elbow*, 15. and then on either side the *Hands*, the *right*, 8. and the *left*, 16.

The *Loyns* are next the Shoulders, with the *Hips*, 18. and in the *Breech*, the *Buttocks*, 19.

These make the *Foot;* the *Thigh*, 21. then the *Leg*, 23. (the *Knee*, being betwixt them, 22.) in which is the *Calf*, 24. with the *Shin*, 25. then the *Ankles*, 26. the *Heel*, 27. and the *Sole*, 28. in the very end, the great *Toe*, 29. with four (other) *Toes*.

Anterior pars Colli (quod desit in *Axillas*, 2.) est *Jugulum*, 3. posterior *Cervix*, 4.

Pectus, 5. est ante; *Dorsum*, 6. retro; Fœminis sunt in illo binæ *Mammæ*, 7. cum *Papillis*.

Sub pectore est *Venter*, 9. in ejus medio, *Umbelicus*, 10. subtus *Inguen*, 11. & *pudenda*.

Scapulæ, 12. sunt a tergo, â quibus pendent *humeri*, 13. ab his *Brachia*, 14. cum *Cubito*, 15. inde ad utrumque Latus, *Manus*, *Dextera*, 8. & *Sinistra*, 16.

Lumbi, 17. excipiunt Humeros, cum *Coxis*, 18. & *in Podice*, (culo) *Nates*, 19.

Absolvunt Pedem ; *Femur*, 21. tum *Crus*, 23. (*Genu*, 22. intermedio.)

in quo *Sura*, 24. cum *Tilia*, 25. abhinc *Tali*, 26. *Calx*, (Calcaneum) 27. & *Solum*, 28. in extremo *Hallux*, 29. cum quatuor *Digitis*.

XXXIX.

The Head and the Hand.   Caput & Manus.

In the *Head* are	In *Capite* sunt
the *Hair*, 1.	*Capillus*, 1.
(which is combed	(qui pectitur
with a *Comb*, 2.)	*Pectine*, 2.)
two *Ears*, 3.	*Aures*, 3. binæ,
the *Temples*, 4.	& *Tempora*, 4.
and the *Face*, 5.	*Facies*, 5.
In the Face are	In facie sunt
the *Fore-head*, 6.	*Frons*, 6.
both the *Eyes*, 7.	*Oculus*, 7. uterque,
the *Nose*, 8.	*Nasus*, 8.
(with two *Nostrils*)	(cum duabus *Naribus*)
the *Mouth*, 9.	*Os*, 9.
the *Cheeks*, 10.	*Genæ*, (Malæ) 10.
and the *Chin*, 13.	& *Mentum*, 13.
The *Mouth* is fenced	Os septum est
with a *Mustacho*, 11.	*Mystace*, 11.
and *Lips*, 12.	& *Labiis*, 12.

A *Tongue* and a *Palate*, | *Lingua* cum *Palato*,
and *Teeth*, 16. | *Dentibus*, 16.
in the *Cheek-bone*. | in *Maxilla*.

A Man's Chin | Mentum virile
is covered with a *Beard*,14. | tegitur *Barba*, 14.
and the Eye | Oculos vero
(in which is the *White* | (in quo *Albugo*
and the *Apple*) | & *Pupilla*)
with *eye-lids*, | *palpæbris*,
and an *eye-brow*, 15. | & *supercilio*, 15.

The *Hand* being closed | *Manus* contracta,
is a *Fist*, 17. | *Pugnus*, 17. est
being open is a *Palm*, 18. | aperta, *Palma*, 18.
in the midst, is the *hollow*, | in medio *Vola*, 19.
19. of the Hand. |
the extremity is the | extremitas,
Thumb, 20. | *Pollex*, 20.
with four *Fingers*, | cum quatuor *Digitis*,
the *Fore-finger*, 21. | *Indice*, 21.
the *Middle-finger*, 22. | *Mediô*, 22.
the *Ring-finger*, 23. | *Annulari*, 23.
and the *Little-finger*, 24. | & *Auriculari*, 24.

In every one are | In quolibet sunt
three *joynts*, a. b. c. | *articuli* tres, a. b. c.
and as many *knuckles*, d.e.f. | & totidem *Condyli*, d. e. f.
with a *Nail*, 25. | cum *Ungue*, 25.

The Flesh and Bowels. XL Caro & Viscera.

In the *Body* are the *Skin* with the *Membranes*, the *Flesh* with the *Muscles*, the *Chanels*, the *Gristles*, the *Bones* and the *Bowels*.	In *Corpore* sunt *Cutis* cum *Membranis*, *Caro* cum *Musculis*, *Canales*, *Cartilagines*, *Ossa* & *Viscera*.
The *Skin*, 1. being pull'd off, the *Flesh*, 2. appeareth, not in a continual lump, but being distributed, as it were in stuft puddings, which they call *Muscles*, whereof there are reckoned four hundred and five, being the Chanels of the *Spirits*, to move the *Members*.	*Cute*, 1. detractâ, *Caro*, 2. apparet, non continuâ massâ, sed distributa, tanquam in farcimina, quos vocant *Musculos*, quorum numerantur *quadringenti quinque*, canales *Spirituum*, ad movendum *Membra*.
The *Bowels* are the inward *Members*:	*Viscera* sunt *Membra* interna :
As in the Head, the *Brains*, 3. being compassed about with a *Skull*, and	Ut in Capite, *Cerebrum*, 3. circumdatum *Cranio*, &

F

the *Skin* which covereth the *Skull.*

In the Breast, the *Heart,* 4. covered with a thin *Skin* about it, and the *Lungs,* 5. breathing to and fro.

In the *Belly,* the *Stomach,* 6. and the *Guts,* 7. covered with a *Caul.* The *Liver,* 8. and in the left side opposite against it, the *Milt,* 9. the two *Kidneys,* 10. and the *Bladder,* 11.

The Breast is divided from the Belly by a thick Membrane, which is called the *Mid-riff,* 12.

Pericranio.

In Pectore, *Cor,* 4. obvolutum *Pericardio,* & *Pulmo,* 5. respirans.

In *Ventre,* *Ventriculus,* 6. & *Intestina,* 7. obducta *Omento.* *Jecur,* (Hepar) 8. & à sinistro oppositus ei *Lien,* 9. duo *Renes,* 10. cum *Vesica,* 11.

Pectus dividitur à Ventre crassâ Membranâ, quæ vocatur *Diaphragma,* 12.

The Chanels and Bones.   XLI.   Canales & Ossa.

The Chanels of the Body are   Canales Corporis sunt

the *Veins*, carrying
the Blood from the Liver;
The *Arteries* (carrying)
Heart and *Life* from the
Heat;
The *Nerves* (carrying)
Sense and Motion
throughout the Body from
the *Brain.*
You shall find these
three, 1. everywhere
joined together.
Besides, from the Mouth
into the Stomach is
the *Gullet,* 2. the
way of the meat and drink;
and by it to the Lights,the
Wezand, 5. for breathing;
from the Stomach to the
Anus is a great *Intestine,* 3.
to purge out the *Ordure;*
from the Liver to the
Bladder, the *Ureter,* 4.
for making water.
The *Bones* are
in the Head, the *Skull,* 6.
the two *Cheek-bones,* 7.
with thirty-two *Teeth,* 8.
Then the *Back-bone,* 9.
the Pillar of the Body,
consisting of thirty-four
turning *Joints,* that the
Body may bend it self.
The *Ribs,* 10. whereof
there are twenty-four.
The *Breast-bone,* 11.
the two *Shoulder-blades,* 12.
the *Buttock-bone,* 13.
the *bigger Bone* in the
Arm, 15. and
the *lesser Bone* in the Arm.

Venæ deferentes
Sanguinem ex Hepate;
Arteriæ, Calorem
& *Vitam è Corde;*

Nervi, Sensum
et Motum, per
Corpus a *Cerebro.*

Invenies hæc tria, 1.
ubique sociata.

Porrò, ab Ore
in Ventriculum
Gula, 2.
via cibi ac potus; &
juxta hanc, ad Pulmonem
*Guttur,*5. pro respiratione;
à ventriculo ad Anum
Colon, 3.
ad excernendum *Stercus;*
ab Hepate ad Vesicam,
Ureter, 4.
reddendæ urinæ.
Ossa sunt
in Capite, *Calvaria,* 6.
duæ *Maxillæ,* 7. cum
XXXII. *Dentibus,* 8.
Tum, *Spina dorsi,* 9.
columna Corporis,
constans ex XXXIV.
Vertebris, ut Corpus
queat flectere se
Costæ, 10.
quarum viginti quatuor.
Os Pectoris, 11.
duæ *Scapulæ,* 12.
Os sessibuli, 13.
Lacerti, 15.

& *Ulna.*

The *Thigh-bone*, 14.
the foremost, 16.
and the hindmost Bone,
in the Leg, 17.

Tibia, 14.
Fibula, 16. anterior,
& posterior, 17.

The Bones of the Hand,
18. are thirty-four, and
of the Foot, 19. thirty.

Ossa Manûs, 18.
sunt triginta quatuor,
Pedis, 19. triginta.

The *Marrow* is in the
Bones.

Medulla est in Ossibus,

XLII.
The Outward and Inward Senses.

Sensus externi & interni.

There are five outward
Senses ;

Sunt quinque externi
Sensus ;

The *Eye*, 1. seeth Col-
ours, what is white or
black, green or blew,
red or yellow.

Oculus, 1. videt *Colores*,
quid album vel atrum,
viride vel cœruleum,
rubrum aut luteum, sit.

The *Ear*, 2. heareth
Sounds, both natural,
Voices and Words;
and artificial,

Auris, 2. audit *Sonos*,
tum naturales,
Voces & Verba;
tum artificiales,

Musical Tunes.

The *Nose*, 3. scenteth smells and stinks.

The *Tongue*, 4. with the roof of the Mouth tastes *Savours*, what is sweet or bitter, keen or biting, sower or harsh.

The *Hand*, 5. by touching discerneth the quantity and quality of things; the hot and cold, the moist and dry, the hard and soft, the smooth and rough, the heavy and light.

The inward *Senses* are three.

The *Common Sense*, 7. under the *forepart of the head*, apprehendeth things taken from the outward Senses.

The *Phantasie*, 6. under the *crown of the head* judgeth of those things, thinketh and dreameth,

The *Memory*, 8. under the *hinder part of the head*, layeth up every thing and fetcheth them out: It loseth some, and this is *forgetfulness*.

Sleep, is the rest of the Senses.

Tonos Musicos.

Nasus, 3, *olfacit* odores & fœtores.

Lingua, 4. cum Palato gustat *Sapores*, quid dulce aut amarum, acre aut acidum, acerbum aut austerum.

Manus, 5. tangendo dignoscit quantitatem, & qualitatem rerum ; calidum & frigidum, humidum & siccum, durum & molle, læve & asperum, grave & leve.

Sensus interni sunt tres.

Sensus Communis, 7. sub *sincipite* apprehendit res perceptas a Sensibus externis.

Phantasia, 6. sub *vertice*, dijudicat res istas, cogitat, somniat.

Memoria, 8. sub *occipitio*, recondit singula & depromit : deperdit quædam, & hoc est *oblivio*.

Somnus, est requies Sensuum.

The Soul of Man.　　XLIII.　　Anima hominis.

The *Soul* is the Life of the Body, one in the whole.	*Anima* est vita corporis, una in toto.
Only *Vegetative* in *Plants;*	Tantùm *Vegetativa* in *Plantis*;
Withal *Sensitive* in *Animals;*	Simul *Sensitiva* in *Animalibus;*
And also rational in *Men.*	Etiam *Rationalis* in *Homine.*
This consisteth in three things;	Hæc consistet in tribus:
In the *Understanding,* whereby it judgeth and understandeth a thing good and evil, or true, or apparent.	In *Mente* (Intellectu) quâ cognoscit, & intelligit, bonum ac malum, vel verum, vel apparens.
In the *Will,* whereby it chooseth, and desireth, or rejecteth, and misliketh a thing known.	In *Voluntate,* quâ eligit, & concupiscit, aut rejicit, & aversatur cognitum.
In the *Mind,* whereby it pursueth	In *Animo,* quo prosequitur

the Good chosen or avoid-
eth the Evil rejected.

Bonum electum,
vel fugit Malum rejectum.

Hence is *Hope* and *Fear*
in the desire,
and dislike.

Hinc *Spes* & *Timor*,
in cupidine,
& aversatione :

Hence is *Love* and *Joy*,
in the Fruition :

Hinc *Amor* & *Gaudium*,
in fruitione :

But *Anger* and *Grief*,
in suffering.

Sed *Ira* ac *Dolor*,
in passione.

The true judgment of a
thing is *Knowledge ;*
the false, is *Error*,
Opinion and *Suspicion.*

Vera cognitio rei,
est *Scientia ;*
falsa, *Error*,
Opinio, Suspicio.

XLIV.

Deformed and Monstrous People.

Deformes & Monstrosi.

Monstrous and *de-
formed* People are those
which differ in the Body
from the ordinary shape,

Monstrosi,
& *deformes* sunt
abeuntes corpore
à communi formâ,

as the huge *Gyant*, 1.	ut sunt, immanis *Gigas*,
the little *Dwarf*, 2.	nanus (*Pumilio*), 2.
One with *two Bodies*, 3.	*Bicorpor*, 3.
One with *two Heads*, 4.	*Biceps*, 4.
and such like Monsters.	& id genus monstra.
Amongst these are reck-	His accensentur,
oned, The *jolt-headed*, 5.	*Capito*, 5.
The great *nosed*, 6.	*Naso*, 6.
The *blubber-lipped*, 7.	*Labeo*, 7.
The *blub-cheeked*, 8.	*Bucco*, 8.
The *goggle-eyed*, 9.	*Strabo*, 9.
The *wry-necked*, 10.	*Obstipus*, 10.
The *great-throated*, 11.	*Strumosus*, 11.
The *Crump-backed*, 12.	*Gibbosus*, 12.
The *Crump-footed*, 13.	*Loripes*, 13.
The *steeple-crowned*, 15.	*Cilo*, 15.
add to these	adde
The *Bald-pated*, 14.	*Calvastrum*, 14.

XLV.

The Dressing of Gardens.	Hortorum cultura.

We have seen Man:	Vidimus hominem :
Now let us go on to Man's	Jam pergamus

living, and to *Handy-craft-Trades*, which tend to it.

The first and most ancient *sustenance*, were the *Fruits of the Earth*.

Hereupon the first labour of Adam, was *the dressing of a garden*.

The *Gardener*, 1. diggeth in a *Garden-plot*, with a *Spade*, 2. or *Mattock*, 3. and maketh *Beds*, 4. and places wherein to plant *Trees*, 5. on which he setteth *Seeds* and *Plants*.

The *Tree-Gardener*, 6. planteth Trees, 7. in an *Orchard*, and grafteth *Cyons*, 8. in *Stocks*, 9.

He fenceth his Garden, either by care, with a *mound*, 10. or a *Stone-wall*, 11. or a *rail*, 12. or *Pales*, 13. or a *Hedge*, 14. made of *Hedge-stakes*, and *bindings*;

Or by Nature, with *Brambles* and *Bryers*, 15.

It is beautified with *Walks*, 16. and *Galleries*, 17.

It is watered with *Fountains*, 18. and a *Watering-pot*, 19.

ad *Victum* hominis, & ad *Artes Mechanicas*, quæ huc faciunt.

Primus & antiquissimus *Victus*, erant *Fruges Terræ*.

Hinc primus Labor Adami, *Horti cultura*.

Hortulanus (Olitor), 1. fodit in *Viridario*, *Ligone*, 2. aut *Bipalio*, 3. facitque *Pulvinos*, 4. ac *Plantaria*, 5.

quibus inserit *Semina* & *Plantas*.

Arborator, 6. plantat Arbores, 7. in *Pomario*, inseritque *Surculos*, 8. *Viviradicibus*, 9.

Sepit hortum vel Cura, *Muro*, 10. aut *Macerie*, 11. aut *Vacerra*, 12. aut *Plancis*, 13. aut *Sepe*, 14. flexâ è *sudibus* & *vitilibus*;

Vel Natura *Dumis* & *Vepribus*, 15.

Ornatur *Ambulacris*, 16. & *Pergulis*, 17.

Rigatur *Fontanis*, 18. & *Harpagio*, 19.

Husbandry.   XLVI.   Agricultura.

The *Plow-man*, 1.	*Arator*, 1.
yoketh *Oxen*, 3.	jungit *Boves*, 3.
to a *Plough*, 2.	*Aratro*, 2.
and holding the *Plow-stilt*,	& tenens *Stivam*, 4.
4. in his left hand,	lævâ,
and the *Plow-staff*, 5.	*Rallum*, 5.
in his right hand,	dextrâ,
with which he removeth	quâ amovet
Clods, 6.	*Glebas*, 6.
he cutteth the Land,	scindit terram
(which was manured afore	(stercoratam antea
with *Dung*, 8.)	*Fimo*, 8.)
with a *Share*, 7.	*Vomere*, 7.
and a *Coulter*,	et *Dentali*,
and maketh *furrows*, 9.	facitque *Sulcos*, 9.
Then he *soweth*	Tum *seminat*
the *Seed*, 10.	*Semen*, 10.
and harroweth it in	& inoccat
with a *Harrow*, 11.	*Occâ*, 11.
The *Reaper*, 12.	*Messor*, 12.
sheareth the ripe corn	metit fruges maturas
with a *Sickle*, 13. gather-	*Falce messoris*, 13.
eth up the *handfuls*, 14.	colligit *Manipulos*, 14.

and bindeth the *Sheaves*, 15.	& colligat *Mergetes*, 15.
The *Thrasher*, 16.	*Tritor*, 16.
thrasheth Corn	triturat frumentum
on the *Barn-floor*, 17.	in *Area Horrei*, 17.
with a *Flayl*, 18. tosseth	*Flagello* (tribula), 18.
it in a *winnowing-basket*, 19.	jactat *ventilabro*, 19.
and so when the *Chaff*,	atque ita *Paleâ*
and the *Straw*, 20.	& *Stramine*, 20.
are separated from it, he	separatâ,
putteth it into *Sacks*, 12.	congerit in *Saccos*, 21.
The *Mower*, 22.	*Fœniseca*, 22.
maketh *Hay* in a *Meadow*,	facit *Fœnum* in *Prato*,
cutting down *Grass*	desecans *Gramen*
with a *Sithe*, 23.	*Falce fœnaria*, 23.
and raketh it together	corraditque
with a *Rake*, 24. and	*Rastro*, 24.
maketh up *Cocks*, 26.	componit *Acervos*, 26.
with a *fork*, 25, and	*Furca*, 25. &
carrieth it on *Carriages*, 27.	convehit *Vehibus*, 27.
into the *Hay-barn*, 28.	in *Fœnile*, 28.

Grasing.	XLVII.	Pecuaria.

Tillage of ground,
and *keeping Cattle,*
was in old time the care
of Kings and Noble-men ;
at this Day only of the
meanest sort of People.

The *Neat-heard,* 1.
calleth out the *Heards,* 2.
out of the *Beast-houses,* 3.
with a *Horn,* 4.
and driveth them to feed.

The *Shepherd,* 5.
feedeth his *Flock,* 6.
being furnished with a
Pipe, 7. and a *Scrip,* 8.
and a *Sheep-hook,* 9.
having with him a great
Dog, 10.
fenced with a *Collar,* 11.
against the *Wolves.*

Swine, 12. are
fed out of a *Swine-Trough.*

The *Farmer's Wife,* 13.
milketh the *Udders*
of the *Cow,* 15.
at the *Cratch,* 15.
over a *milk-pale,* 16.
and maketh *Butter*
of *Cream*
in a *Churn,* 17.
and *Cheeses,* 18.
of *Curds.*

The *Wool,* 19.
is shorn from *Sheep,*
whereof several *Garments*
are made.

Cultus Agrorum,
& *res pecuaria,*
antiquissimis temporibus,
erat cura Regum,Heroum;
hodie tantum infirmæ
Plebis,

Bubulcus, 1.
evocat *Armenta,* 2.
è *Bovilibus,* 3.
Buccina (Cornu), 4,
& ducit pastum.

Opilio (Pastor), 5.
pascit *Gregem,* 6.
instructus *Fistula,* 7.
& *Pera,* 8.
ut & *Pedo,* 9.
habens secum *Molossum,*
10.
munitum *Millo,* 11.
contra Lupos.

Sues, 12. sagi-
nantur ex *aqualiculo haræ.*

Villica, 13.
mulget *Ubera*
vaccæ, 14.
ad *Præsepe,* 15.
super *mulctra,* 16.
et facit *Butyrum*
è *flore lactis,*
in *Vase butyraceo,* 17.
et *Caseos,* 18.
è *Coagulo.*

Lana, 19.
detondetur *Ovibus,*
ex quâ variæ *Vestes*
conficiuntur.

XLVIII.

The making of Honey.   Mellificium.

The *Bees* send out
a *swarm*, 1. and set over
it a *Leader*, 2.

That swarm
being ready to fly away is
recalled by the Tinkling
of a *brazen Vessel*, 3.
and is put up
into a new *Hive*, 4.

They make little *Cells*
with six corners, 5. and
fill them with *Honey-dew*,
and make *Combs*, 6.
out of which the *Honey*
runneth, 7.

The *Partitions* being
melted by fire,
turn into *Wax*, 8.

Apes emittunt
Examen, 1. adduntque illi
Ducem (Regem), 2.

Examen illud,
avolaturum,
revocatur tinnitu
Vasis ænei, 3.
& includitur
novo *Alveari*, 4.

Struunt *Cellulas*
sexangulares, 5.
et complent eas *Melligine*,
& faciunt *Favos*, 6.
è quibus *Mel*
effluit, 7.

Crates
liquati igne
abeunt in *Ceram*, 8.

Grinding. XLIX. Molitura

In a *Mill*, 1.
a Stone, 2. runneth
upon a stone, 3.

A *Wheel*, 4.
turning them about'
and grindeth Corn poured
in by a *Hopper*, 5.
and parteth the *Bran*, 6.
falling into the *Trough*, 7.
from the *Meal* slipping
through a *Bolter*, 8.

Such a Mill was first
a *Hand-mill*, 9.
then a *Horse-mill*, 10.
then a *Water-mill*, 11.
then a *Ship-mill*, 12.
and at last a *Wind-mill*, 13.

In *Mola*,
Lapis, 2. currit
super lapidem, 3,

Rota, 4.
circumagente, et
conterit grana infusa
per *Infundibulum*, 5.
separatque *Furfurem*, 6.
decidentem in *Cistam*, 7.
à *Farina* (Polline)
elabente per *Excussorium*, 8.

Talis Mola primùm fuit
Manuaria, 9.
deinde *Jumentaria*, 10.
tum *Aquatica*, 11.
& *Navalis*, 12. tandem,
Alata (pneumatica), 13.

Bread-baking.   L.   Panificium.

The *Baker*, 1.	*Pistor*, 1.

The *Baker*, 1.
sifteth the *Meal*
in a *Rindge*, 2.
and putteth it into the
Kneading-trough, 3.

Then he poureth water
to it and maketh *Dough*, 4.
and kneadeth it
with a *wooden slice*, 5.

Then he maketh
Loaves, 6. *Cakes*, 7.
Cimnels, 8. *Rolls*, 9, &c.

Afterwards he setteth
them on a *Peel*, 10.
and putteth them thorow
the *Oven-mouth*, 12.
into the *Oven*, 11.

But first he pulleth out
the fire and the Coals with
a *Coal-rake*, 13.

Pistor, 1.
cernit *Farinam*
Cribo, 2. (pollinario)
& indit *Mactræ*, 3.

Tum affundit aquam,
& facit *Massam*, 4.
depsitque
spatha, 5. ligneâ.

Dein format
Panes, 6. *Placentas*, 7.
Similas, 8. *Spiras*, 9. &c.

Post imponit
Palæ, 10.
& ingerit *Furno*, 11.

per *Præfurnium*, 12.
Sed priùs eruit
ignem & Carbones
Rutabulo, 13.

which he layeth on a heap underneath, 14.

And thus is *Bread* baked, having the *Crust* without, 15. and the *Crumb* within, 16.

quos congerit infra, 14.

Et sic *Panis* pinsitur habens extra *Crustam*, 15. intus *Micam*, 16.

Fishing.   LI.   Piscatio.

The *Fisher-man*, 1. catcheth fish, either on the Shoar, wlth an *Hook*, 2. which hangeth by a *Line* from the *angling-rod*, on which the *Bait* sticketh; or with a *Cleek-net*, 3. which hangeth on a *Pole*, 4. is put into the Water; or in a *Boat*, 5. with a *Trammel-net*, 6. or with a *Wheel*, 7. which is laid in the Water by Night.

Piscator, 1. captat pisces, sive in littore, *Hamo*, 2. qui pendet *filo* ab *arundine*, & cui *Esca* inhæret; sive *Fundâ*, 3. quæ pendens *Pertica*, 4. immittitur aquæ; sive in *Cymba*, 5. *Reti*, 6. sive *Nassa*, 7. quæ demergitur per Noctem.

Fowling.   LII.   Aucupium.

The *Fowler*, 1. maketh a *Bed*, 2, spreadeth a *Bird-net*, 3. throweth a *Bait*, 4. upon it, and hiding himself in a *Hut*, 5. he allureth Birds, by the chirping of *Lure-birds*, which partly hop upon the Bed, 6. and are partly shut in *Cages*, 7. and thus he entangleth Birds that fly over, in his net whilst they settle themselves down.

Or he setteth *Snares*, 8. on which they hang and strangle themselves :

Or setteth *Lime-twigs*, 9. on a *Perch*, 10.

Auceps, 1. exstruit *Aream*, 2. superstruit illi *Rete* aucupatorium, 3. obsipat *Escam*, 4. & abdens se in *Latibulo*, 5. allicit Aves, cantu *Illicum*, qui partim in Area currunt, 6. partim inclusi sunt *Caveis*, 7. atque ita obruit transvolantes Aves Reti, dum se demittunt :

Aut tendit *Tendiculas*, 8. quibus suspendunt & suffocant seipsas :

Aut exponit *Viscatos calamos*, 9. *Amiti*, 10.

G

upon which if they sit they enwrap their Feathers, so that they cannot fly away, and fall down to the ground.	quibus si insident, implicant pennas, ut nequeant avolare, & decidunt in terram.
Or he catcheth them with a *Pole*, 11. or a *Pit-fall*, 12.	Aut captat *Perticâ*, 11. vel *Decipulâ*, 12.

Hunting.	LIII.	Venatus.

The *Hunter*, 1. hunteth wild Beasts whilst he besetteth a Wood with *Toyls*, 2. stretched out upon *Shoars*, 3.	*Venator*, 1. venatur Feras, dum cingit Sylvam, *Cassibus*, 2. tentis super *Varos*, 3. (furcillas.)
The *Beagle*, 4. tracketh the wild Beast or findeth him out by the scent; the *Tumbler*, or *Greyhound*, 5. pursueth it.	*Canis sagax*, 4. vestigat Feram, aut indagat odoratu; *Vertagus*, 5. persequitur.
The *Wolf*, falleth in a *Pit*, 6.	*Lupus*, incidit in *Foveam*, 6.

the *Stag*, 7. as he runneth away, into *Toyls*.	fugiens *Cervus*, 7. in *Plagas*.
The *Boar*, 8. is struck through with a *Hunting-spear*, 9.	*Aper*, 8. transverberatur *Venabulo*, 9.
The *Bear*, 10. is bitten by Dogs, and is knocked with a *Club*, 11.	*Ursus*, 10. mordetur à Canibus, & tunditur *Clavâ*, 11.
If any thing get away, it escapeth, 12. as here a *Hare* and a *Fox*.	Si quid effugit, evadit, 12. ut hic *Lepus* & *Vulpes*.

Butchery.	LIV.	Lanionia.

The *Butcher*, 1. killeth *fat Cattle*, 2. (The *Lean*, 3. are not fit to eat.)	*Lanio*, 1. mactat *Pecudem altilem*, 2. (*Vescula*, 3. non sunt vescenda.)
He knocketh them down with an *Ax*, 4. or cutteth their Throat.	Prosternit *Clavâ*, 4. vel jugulat.

with a *Slaughter-knife*, 5.	*Cunaculo*, 5.
he flayeth them, 6.	excoriat (deglubit,) 6.
and cutteth them in pieces,	dissecatque
and hangeth out the flesh	& exponit carnes,
to sell in the *Shambles*, 7.	venum in *Macello*, 7.
He dresseth a *Swine*, 8.	Glabrat *Suem*, 8.
with fire	igne,
or scaldĭng water, 9.	vel aquâ fervidâ, 9.
and maketh *Gamons*, 10.	& facit *Pernas*, 10.
Pistils, 11.	*Petasones*, 11.
and *Flitches*, 12.	& *Succidias*, 12.
Besides several *Puddings*,	Prætereâ *Farcimina*
Chitterlings, 13.	varia, *Faliscos*, 13.
Bloodings, 14.	*Apexabones*, 14.
Liverings, 15.	*Tomacula*, 15.
Sausages, 16.	*Botulos*, (Lucanicas) 16.
The *Fat*, 17. and	*Adeps*, 17. &
Tallow, 18. are melted.	*Sebum*, 18. eliquantur.

Cookery.	LV.	Coquinaria.

The Yeoman of the Larder,	*Promus Condus*, 1.
1. bringeth forth *Provision*,	profert *Obsonia*, 2.
2. out of the *Larder*, 3.	è *Penu*, 3.

The *Cook*, 4. taketh them and maketh *several Meats*.

He first pulleth off the Feathers and draweth the Gutts out of the *Birds*, 5.

He scaleth and splitteth *Fish*, 6.

He draweth some flesh with *Lard*, by means of a *Larding-needle*, 7.

He caseth *Hares*, 8. then he boileth them in *Pots*, 9. and *Kettles*, 10. on the *Hearth*, 11. and scummeth them with a *Scummer*, 12.

He seasoneth things that are boyled with Spices, which he poundeth with a *Pestil*, 14. in a *Morter*, 13. or grateth with a *Grater*,15.

He roasteth some on *Spits*, 16. and with a *Jack*, 17. or upon a *Grid-iron*, 18.

Or fryeth them in a *Frying-pan*, 19. upon a *Brand-iron*, 20.

Kitchen utensils besides are,
a *Coal-rake*, 21.
a *Chafing-dish*, 22.
a *Trey*, 23.
(in which *Dishes*, 24. and *Platters*, 25. are washed),
a pair of *Tongs*, 26.
a *Shredding-knife*, 27.
a *Colander*, 28.
a *Basket*, 29.
and a *Besom*, 30.

Coquus, 4. accipit ea & coquit *varia Esculenta*.

Prius deplumat, & exenterat *Aves*, 5.

Desquamat & exdorsuat *Pisces*, 6.

Trajectat quasdem carnes *Lardo*, ope *Creacentri*, 7.

Lepores, 8. exuit, tum elixat *Ollis*, 9. & *Cacabis*, 10. in *Foco*, 11. & despumat *Lingula*, 12.

Condit elixata, Aromatibus, quæ comminuit *Pistillo*, 14. in *Mortario*, 13. aut terit *Radulâ*, 15.

Quædam assat *Verubus*, 16. & *Automato*, 17. vel super *Craticulum*, 18.

Vel frigit *Sartagine*, 19. super *Tripodem*, 20.

Vasa Coquinaria præterea sunt,
Rutabulum, 21.
Foculus (Ignitabulum), 22.
Trua, 23.
(in quà *Catini*, 24. & *Patinæ*, 25. eluuntur)
Forceps, 26.
Culter incisorius, 27.
Qualus, 28.
Corbis, 29.
& *Scopa*, 30.

The Vintage.   LVI.   Vindemia.

Wine groweth	*Vinum* crescit
in the *Vine-yard*, 1.	in *Vinea*, 1.
where *Vines* are propa-	ubi *Vites* propagantur,
gated and tyed with Twigs	& alligantur viminibus
to *Trees*, 2.	ad *Arbores*, 2.
or to *Props*, 3.	vel ad *Palos* (ridicas), 3.
or *Frames*, 4.	vel ad *Juga*, 4
When the time of Grape-	Cùm tempus vindemi-
gathering is come, they	andi adest, abscindunt
cut off the *Bunches*,	*Botros*,
and carry them in	& comportant
Measures of three Bushels, 5.	*Trimodiis*, 5.
and throw them into a *Vat*,	conjiciuntque in *Lacum*, 6.
6. and tread them	calcant
with their *Feet*, 7.	*Pedibus*. 7.
or stamp them	aut tundunt
with a *Wooden-Pestil*, 8.	*Ligneo Pilo*, 8.
and squeeze out the juice	& exprimunt succum
in a *Wine-press*, 9.	*Torculari*, 9.
which is called *Must*, 11.	qui dicitur *Mustum*, 11.

and

(71)

and being received	& exceptum
in a great *Tub*, 10.	*Orcâ*, 10.
it is poured into	infunditur
Hogsheads, 12.	*Vasis* (Doliis), 12.
it is stopped up, 15.	operculatur, 15.
and being laid close in *Cel-*	& abditum in *Cellis*,
lars upon *Settles*, 14.	super *Cantherios*, 14.
it becometh *Wine*.	abit in *Vinum*.
It is drawn out of the	Promitur e *Dolio*
Hogshead, with a *Cock*, 13.	*Siphone*, 13.
or *Faucet*, 16.	aut *Tubulo*, 16.
(in which is a *Spigot*) the	(in quo est *Epistomium*)
Vessel being unbunged.	Vase relito.

Brewing.	LVII.	Zythopoie.

Where *Wine* is not to be	Ubi *Vinum* non habetur,
had they drink *Beer*,	bibitur *Cerevisia* (Zythus),
which is brewed of *Malt*, 1.	quæ coquitur ex *Byne*, 1.
and *Hops*, 2.	& *Lupulo*, 2.
in a *Caldron*, 3.	in *Aheno*, 3.
afterwards it is poured	post effunditur
into *Vats*, 4.	in *Lacus*, 4.

and when it is cold,	& frigefactum.
it is carried in *Soes*, 5,	defertur *Labris*, 5.
into the *Cellar*, 6.	in *Cellaria*, 6.
and is put into Vessels.	& intunditur vasibus.
Brandy-wine,	*Vinum sublimatum*,
extracted by the power of	extractum vi Caloris
heat from dregs of Wine in	e fecibus Vini in *Aheno*, 7.
a *Pan*, 7. over which a *Lim-*	cui *Alembicum*, 8.
beck, 8. is placed,	superimpositum est.
droppeth through a *Pipe*, 9.	destillat per *Tubum*, 9.
into a *Glass*.	in *Vitrum*.
Wine and Beer when	Vinum & Cerevisia, cum
they turn sowre, become	acescunt, fiunt *Acetum*.
Vinegar.	
Of Wine and	Ex Vino & Melle fac-
Honey they make *Mead*.	iunt *Mulsum*.

A Feast.   LVIII.   Convivium.

When a *Feast*	Cum *Convivium*
is made ready,	apparatur,
the table is covered	Mensa sternitur
with a *Carpet*, 1.	*Tapetibus*, 1.

English	Latin
and a *Table-cloth*, 2.	& *Mappa*, 2.
by the *Waiters*,	à *Tricliniariis*,
who besides lay	qui præterea opponunt
the *Trenchers*, 3.	*Discos* (Orbes), 3.
Spoons, 4.	*Cochlearia*, 4.
Knives, 5.	*Cultros*, 5.
with little *Forks*, 6.	cum *Fuscinulis*, 6.
Table-napkins, 7.	*Mappulas*, 7.
Bread, 8.	*Panem*, 8.
with a *Salt-seller*, 9.	cum *Salino*, 9.
Messes are brought	*Fercula* inferuntur
in *Platters*, 10.	in *Patinis*, 10.
a *Pie*, 19. on a *Plate*.	*Artocrea*, 19. in *Lance*.
The Guests being	Convivæ introducti
brought in by the *Host*, 11.	ab *Hospite*, 11.
wash their Hands	abluunt manus
out of a *Laver*, 12.	è *Gutturnio*, 12.
or *Ewer*, 14.	vel *Aquali*, 14.
over a *Hand-basin*, 13.	super *Malluvium*, 13.
or *Bowl*, 15.	aut *Pelvim*, 15.
and wipe them	terguntque
on a *Hand-towel*, 16.	*Mantili*, 16.
then they sit at the Table	tum assident Mensæ
on *Chairs*, 17.	per *Sedilia*, 17.
The *Carver*, 18.	*Structor*, 18.
breaketh up the good	deartuat dapes,
Cheer, and divideth it.	& distribuit.
Sauces are set amongst	*Embammata* interponuntur
Roast-meat, in Sawcers, 20.	*Assutaris* in Scutellis, 20.
The *Butler*, 21.	*Pincerna*, 21. infundit
filleth *strong Wine*	*Temetum*,
out of a *Cruise*, 25.	ex *Urceo*, 25.
or *Wine-pot*, 26.	vel *Cantharo*, 26.
or *Flagon*, 27.	vel *Lagena*, 27.
into *Cups*, 22.	in *Pocula*, 22.
or *Glasses*, 23.	vel *Vitrea*, 23.
which stand	quæ extant
on a *Cupboard*, 24. and	in *abaco*, 24.
he reacheth them to the	& porrigit,
Master of the Feast, 28. who	*Convivatori*, 28.
drinketh to his *Guests*.	qui propinat *Hospitibus*.

The Dressing of Line.　　LIX.　　Tractatio Lini.

Line and *Hemp*	*Linum* & *Cannabis*,
being rated in water,	macerata aquis,
and dryed again, 1.	et siccata rursum, 1.
are braked	contunduntur
with a *wooden Brake*, 2.	*Frangibulo ligneo*, 2.
where the *Shives*, 3. fall	ubi *Cortices*, 3. decidunt
down, then they are hec-	tum carminantur
kled with an *Iron Heckle*, 4.	*Carmine ferreo*, 4.
where the *Tow*, 5.	ubi *Stupa*, 5.
is parted from it.	separatur.
Flax is tyed to a *Distaff*,	*Linum purum* alligatur
6. by the *Spinster*, 7.	*Colo*, 6. à *Netrice*, 7.
which with her left hand	quæ sinistra
pulleth out the *Thread*, 8.	trahit *Filum*, 8.
and with her right hand	dexterâ, 12.
turneth a *Wheel*, 9.	*Rhombum* (girgillum), 9.
or a *Spindle*, 10. upon	vel *Fusum*, 10.
which is a *Wharl*, 11.	in quo *Verticillus*, 11.
The *Spool* receiveth	*Volva* accipit
the *Thread*, 13.	*Fila*, 13.

which is drawn thence	inde deducuntur
upon a *Yarn-windle*, 14.	in *Alabrum*, 14.
hence either *Clews*, 15.	hinc vel *Glomi*, 15.
are wound up,	glomerantur,
or *Hanks*, 16. are made.	vel *Fasciculi*, 16. fiunt.

Weaving.　　　　　LX.　　　　Textura.

The *Webster*	*Textor*
undoeth the *Clews*, 1.	didücit *Glomos*, 1.
into *Warp*,	in *Stamen*,
and wrappeth it about	& circumvolvit
the *Beam*, 2.	*Jugo*, 2.
and as he sitteth	ac sedens
in his *Loom*, 3.	in *Textrino*, 3.
he treadeth upon the	calcat *Insilia*, 4.
Treddles, 4. with his Feet.	pedibus.
He divideth the *Warp*, 5.	Diducit *Stamen*, 5.
with *Yarn*.	*Liciis*,
and throweth the *Shuttle*, 6.	& trajicit *Radium*, 6.
through, in which is the	in quo est *Trama*,
Woofe, and striketh it close.	ac densat.

with the *Sley*, 7.	*Pectine*, 7.
and so maketh	atque ita conficit
Linen cloth, 8.	*Linteum*, 8.
So also the *Clothier*	Sic etiam *Pannifex*
maketh *Cloth* of *Wool*.	facit *Pannum* è *Lana*.

Linen Cloths.	LXI.	Lintea.

Linnen-webs	*Linteamina*
are bleached in the *Sun*, 1.	insolantur, 1.
with Water poured on	aquâ perfusâ, 2.
them, 2. till they be white.	donec candefiant.
Of them the *Sempster*, 3.	Ex iis *Sartrix*, 3.
soweth *Shirts*, 4.	suit *Indusia*, 4.
Handkirchers, 5.	*Muccinia*, 5.
Bands, 6. *Caps*, &c.	*Collaria*, 6. *Capitia*, &c.
These if they be fouled,	Hæc, si sordidentur
are washed again	lavantur rursum,
by the *Laundress*, 7. in	a *Lotrice*, 7. aquâ,
water, or *Lye* and *Sope*.	sive *Lixivio* ac *Sapone*.

The Taylor.   LXII.   Sartor.

The *Taylor*, 1. cutteth *Cloth*, 2. with *Shears*, 3. and seweth it together with a *Needle* and *double thread*, 4.

Then he presseth the *Seams* with a *Pressing-iron*, 5.   And thus he maketh *Coats*, 6.

with *Plaits*, 7.

in which the *Border*, 8. is below with *Laces*, 9.

Cloaks, 10.

with a *Cape*, 11.

and *Sleeve Coats*, 12.

Doublets, 13.

with *Buttons*, 14.

and *Cuffs*, 15.

Breeches, 16.

sometimes with *Ribbons*, 17.

Stockins, 18.

Gloves, 19.

Sartor, 1. discindit *Pannum*, 2. *Forfice*, 3. consuitque *Acu* & *Filo duplicato*, 4.

Posteâ complanat *Su-turas Ferramento*, 5.

Sicque conficit *Tunicas*, 6.

Plicatas, 7.

in quibus infra est *Fimbria*, 8. cum *Institis*, 9.

Pallia, 10.

cum *Patagio*, 11.

& *Togas Manicatas*, 12.

Thoraces, 13.

cum *Globulis*, 14.

& *Manicis*, 15.

Caligas, 16. aliquando cum *Lemniscis*, 17.

Tibialia, 18.

Chirothecas, 19.

Muntero Caps, 20. &c.	*Amiculum*, 20. &c.
So the *Furrier*	Sic *Pellio*
maketh *Furred Garments*	facit *Pellicia*
of *Furs*.	è *Pellibus*.

The Shoemaker.   LXIII.   Sutor.

The *Shoemaker*, 1.	*Sutor*, 1.
maketh *Slippers*, 7.	conficit *Crepidas* (San-
Shoes, 8.	dalia,) 7. *Calceos*, 8.
(in which is seen	(in quibus spectatur
above, the *Upper-leather*,	superne *Obstragulum*,
beneath the *Sole*,	inferne *Solea*,
and on both sides	et utrinque
the *Latchets*)	*Ansæ*)
Boots, 9.	*Ocreas*, 9.
and *High Shoes*, 10.	et *Perones*, 10.
of *Leather*, 5.	e *Corio*, 5.
(which is cut with a	(quod discinditur
Cutting-knife), 6.	*Scalpro Sutorio*, 6.)
by means of an *Awl*, 2.	ope *Subulæ*, 2.
and *Lingel*, 3.	et Fili *picati*, 3.
upon a *Last*, 4.	super *Modum*, 4.

The Carpenter.   LXIV.   Faber lignarius.

We have seen Man's food and clothing: now his Dwelling followeth.	Hominis victum & amictum, vidimus: sequitur nunc Domicilium ejus.
At first they dwelt in *Caves*, 1. then in *Booths* or *Huts*, 2. and then again in *Tents*, 3. at the last in *Houses*.	Primò habitabant in *Specubus*, 1. deinde in *Tabernaculis* vel *Tuguriis*, 2. tum etiam in *Tentoriis*, 3. demum in *Domibus*.
The *Woodman* felleth and heweth down *Trees*, 5. with an *Ax*, 4. the *Boughs*, 6. remaining.	*Lignator* sternit & truncat *Arbores*, 5. *Securi*, 4. remanentibus *Sarmentis*, 6.
He cleaveth *Knotty Wood* with a *Wedge*, 7. which he forceth in with a *Beetle*, 8. and maketh *Wood-stacks*, 9.	Findit *Nodosum*, *Lignum Cuneo*, 7. quem adigit *Tudite*, 8. & componit *Strues*, 9.
The *Carpenter* squareth *Timber* with a *Chip-Ax*, 10.	*Faber Lignarius* ascit *Ascia*, 10. *Materiem*,

whence *Chips*, 11. fall, and saweth it with a *Saw*, 12. where the *Saw-dust*, 13. falleth down.	unde *Assulæ*, 11. cadunt, & serrat *Serrâ*, 12. ubi *Scobs*, 13. decidit.
Afterwards he lifteth the *Beam* upon *Tressels*, 14. by the help of a *Pully*, 15. fasteneth it with *Cramp-irons*, 16. and marketh it out with a *Line*, 17.	Post elevat *Tignum* super *Canterios*, 14. ope *Trochleæ*, 15. affigit *Ansis*, 16. & lineat *Amussi*, 17.
Thus he frameth the *Walls* together, 18. and fasteneth the great pieces with *Pins*, 19.	Tum compaginat *Parietes*, 18. & configit trabes *Clavis trabalibus*, 19.

The Mason.   LXV.   Faber Murarius,

The *Mason*, 1. layeth a *Foundation*, and buildeth *Walls*, 2.	*Faber Murarius*, 1. ponit *Fundamentum*, & struit *Muros*, 2.
Either of *Stones* which the *Stone-digger* getteth out of the *Quarry*, 3.	Sive è *Lapidibus*, quos *Lapidarius* eruit in *Lapicidina*, 3.

and the *Stone-cutter*, 4.	& *Latomus*, 4.
squareth by a *Rule*, 5.	conquadrat ad *Normam*, 5.
Or of *Bricks*, 6.	Sive è *Lateribus*, 6.
which are made	qui formantur,
of *Sand* and *Clay*	ex *Arena* & *Luto*,
steeped in water,	aquâ intritis
and are burned in fire.	& excoquuntur igne.
Afterwards he plaister-	Dein crustat
eth it with *Lime*,	*Calce*,
by means of a *Trowel*,	ope *Trullæ*, 7.
and garnisheth with a	& vestit *Tectorio*, 8.
Rough-cast, 8.	

Engines.	LXVI.	Machinæ.

One can carry	Unus potest ferre
as much by thrusting	tantum trudendo
a *Wheel-barrow*, 3.	*Pabonem*, 3.
before him, (having	ante se,
an *Harness*, 4. hanging	(*Ærumna*,
on his neck,) as two men	Suspensâ a Collo) quan-
can carry on a *Colestaff*, 1.	tum duo possunt ferre
or *Hand-barrow*, 2.	*Palangâ*, vel *Feretro*, 2.

H

But he can do more that
rolleth a Weight laid upon
Rollers, 6. with a *Leaver*, 5.

A *Wind-beam*, 7.
is a post, which is
turned by going about it.

A *Crane*, 8.
hath a *Hollow-wheel*,
in which one walking
draweth weights out of a
Ship, or letteth them down
into a Ship.

A *Rammer*, 9.
is used to fasten
Piles, 10.
it is lifted with a Rope
drawn by *Pullies*, 11.
or with hands.
if it have *handles*, 12.

Plus autem potest qui pro-
volvit Molem impositam
Phalangis (Cylindris, 6.)
Vecte, 5.   *Ergata*, 7.
est columella, quæ
versatur circumeundo.

Geranium, 8.
habet *Tympanum*,
cui inambulans quis
extrahit pondera navi,
aut demittit in navem.

Fistuca, 9.
adhibetur ad pangendum
Sublicas, 10.
adtollitur Fune
tracto per *Trochleas*, 11.
vel manibus,
si habet *ansas*, 12.

A House.   LXVII.   Domus.

The *Porch*, 1.
is before the *Door*
of the *House*.

Vestibulum, 1.
est ante *Januam*
Domûs.

The *Door* hath	*Janua* habet
a *Threshold*, 2.	*Limen*, 2.
and a *Lintel*, 3.	& *Superliminare*, 3.
and *Posts*, 4. on both sides.	& *Postes*, 4. utrinque.
The *Hinges*, 5.	*Cardines*, 5.
are upon the right hand,	sunt a dextris,
upon which the *Doors*, 6.	à quibus pendent *Fores*, 6.
hang, the *Latch*, 7.	*Claustrum*, 7.
and the *Bolt*, 8.	aut *Pessulus*, 8.
are on the left hand.	a sinistris.
Before the House	Sub ædibus
is a *Fore-court*, 9.	est *Cavædium*, 9.
with a *Pavement*	*Pavimento*
of *square stones*, 10.	*Tessellato*, 10.
born up with *Pillars*, 11.	fulcitum *Columnis*, 11.
in which is the *Chapiter*, 12.	in quibus *Peristylium*, 12.
and the *Base*, 13.	& *Basis*, 13.
They go up into the up-	Ascenditur in superiores
per Stories by *Greess*, 14.	contignationes per *Scalas*,
and *Winding-stairs*, 15.	14. & *Cocklidia*, 15.
The *Windows*, 16.	*Fenestræ*, 16.
appear on the outside,	apparent extrinsecus,
and the *Grates*, 17.	& *Cancelli* (clathra), 17.
the *Galleries*, 18.	*Pergulæ*, 18.
the *Watertables*, 19.	*Suggrundia*, 19.
the *Butteresses*, 20.	& *Fulcra*, 20.
to bear up the walls.	fulciendis muris.
On the top is the *Roof*, 21.	In summo est *Tectum*, 21.
covered with *Tyles*, 22.	contectum *Imbricibus* (*teg-*
or *Shingles*, 23.	*ulis*), 22. vel *Scandulis*, 23.
which lie upon *Laths*, 24.	quæ incumbunt *Tigillis*,
and these upon *Rafters*, 25.	24. hæc *Tignis*, 25.
The *Eaves*, 26.	*Tecto* adhæret
adhere to the *Roof*.	*Stillicidium*, 26.
The place without a Roof	Locus sine Tecto
is called an *open Gallery*, 27.	dicitur *Subdiale*, 27.
In the Roof are	In Tecto sunt
Jettings out, 28.	*Meniana*, 28.
and *Pinnacles*, 29.	& *Coronides*, 29.

A Mine.   LXVIII.   Metallifodina.

Miners, 1.
go into the *Grave*, 2.
by a *Stick*, 3.
or by *Ladders*, 4.
with *Lanthorns*, 5.
and dig out with a
Pick, 6. the *Oar*,
which being put in *Baskets*,
7. is drawn out with a *Rope*,
8. by means of a *Turn*, 9.
and is carried
to the *Melting-house*, 10.
where it is forced with fire,
that the *Metal* may run
out, 12. the *Dross*, 11. is
thrown aside.

Metalli fossores, 1.
ingrediuntur *Puteum fod-
inæ*, 2. *Bacillo*, 3,
sive *Gradibus*, 4.
cum *Lucernis*, 5.
& effodiunt *Ligone*, 6.
terram Metallicam,
quæ imposita *Corbibus*, 7.
extrahitur *Fune*, 8.
ope *Machinæ tractoriæ*, 9.
& defertur
in *Ustrinam*, 10.
ubi urgetur igne,
ut *Metallum*, 12. profluat
Scoriæ, 11. abjiciuntur
scorsim.

The Blacksmith.   LXIX.   Faber Ferrarius.

The *Blacksmith*, 1.
in his *Smithy* (or Forge), 2.
bloweth the fire
with a *pair of Bellows*, 3.
which he bloweth
with his *Feet*, 4.
and so heateth the *Iron:*

And then he taketh it
out with the *Tongs*, 5.
layeth it upon the *Anvile*, 6.
and striketh it
with an *Hammer*, 7.
where the *sparks*, 8. fly off.

And thus are hammer'd
out, *Nails*, 9.
Horse-shoes, 10.
Cart-strakes, 11.
Chains, 12.
Plates, Locks and *Keys,*
Hinges, &c.

He quencheth hot Irons
in a *Cool-trough.*

Faber ferrarius, 1.
in *Ustrina* (Fabricâ), 2.
inflat ignem
Folle, 3.
quem adtollit
Pede, 4.
atq; ita candefacit *Ferrum:*

Deinde eximit
Forcipe, 5.
imponit *Incudi*, 6.
& cudit
Malleo, 7.
ubi *Stricturæ*, 8. exiliunt.

Et sic excuduntur,
Clavi, 9.
Solea, 10.
Canthi. 11.
Catenæ, 12.
Laminæ, Seræ cum *Clavibus,*
Cardines, &c.

Restinguit cadentia,
Ferramenta in *Lacu.*

LXX.

The Box-maker and the Turner.

Scrinarius & Tornator.

The *Box-maker*, 1.	*Arcularius*, 1.
smootheth *hewen Boards*, 2.	edolat *Asseres*, 2.
with a *Plain*, 3.	*Runcina*, 3.
upon a *work-board*, 4. he	in *Tabula*, 4.
maketh them very smooth	deplanat
with a *little-plain*, 5.	*Planula*, 5.
he boreth them thorow	perforat (terebrat)
with an *Augre*, 6. carv-	*Terebra*, 6.
eth them with a *Knife*, 7.	sculpit *Cultro*, 7.
fasteneth them together	combinat
with *Glew* and *Cramp-Irons*,	*Glutine* & *Subscudibus*, 8.
8. and maketh *Tables*, 9.	& facit *Tabulas*, 9.
Boards, 10.	*Mensas*, 10.
Chests, 11. &c.	*Arcus* (Cistas), 11. &c.
The *Turner*, 12.	*Tornio*, 12.
sitting over the *Treddle*, 13.	sedens in *Insili*, 13.
turneth with a *Throw*, 15.	tornat *Torno*, 15.

upon a *Turner's Bench*, 14.	super *Scamno Tornatorio,*
Bowls, 16. *Tops*, 17,	14. *Globos*, 16. *Conos*, 17.
Puppets, 18. and	*Icunculas*, 18. &
such like *Turners Work.*	similia *Toreumata.*

The Potter.	LXXI.	Figulus.

The *Potter*, 1.	*Figulas*, 1.
sitting over a *Wheel*, 2.	sedens super *Rota*, 2.
maketh *Pots*, 4.	format *Ollas*, 4.
Pitchers, 5.	*Urceos*, 5.
Pipkins, 6.	*Tripodes*, 6.
Platters, 7.	*Patinas*, 7.
Pudding-pans, 8.	*Vasa testacea*, 8.
Juggs, 9.	*Fidelias*, 9.
Lids, 10. &c.	*Opercula*, 10. &c.
of *Potter's Clay*, 3.	ex *Argillâ*, 3.
afterwards he baketh them	postea excoquit
in an *Oven*, 11.	in *Furno*, 11.
and glazeth them	& incrustat
with *White Lead.*	*Lithargyro.*
A broken Pot affordeth	Fracta Olla dat
Pot-sheards, 12.	*Testas*, 12.

The Parts of a House.   LXXII.   Partes Domus

A *House* is divided into inner *Rooms*, such as are the *Entry*, 1. the *Stove*, 2. the *Kitchen*, 3. the *Buttery*, 4. the *Dining Room*, 5. the *Gallery*, 6. the *Bed Chamber*, 7. with a *Privy*, 8. made by it.	*Domus* distinguitur in *Conclavia*, ut sunt *Atrium*, 1. *Hypocaustum*, 2. *Cella Penuaria*, 4. *Cœnaculum*, 5. *Camera*, 6. *Cubiculum*, 7. cum *Secessu* (Latrina), 8. adstructo.
Baskets, 9. are of use for carrying things. and *Chests*, 10. (which are made fast with a *Key*, 11.) for keeping them.	*Corbes*, 9. inserviunt rebus transferendis, *Arcæ*, 10. (quæ *Clavâ*, 11. recluduntur) adfervandis illis.
Under the *Roof*, is the *Floor*, 12.	Sub *Tecto*, est *Solum* (Pavimentum), 12.
In the *Yard*, 13. is a *Well*, 14. a *Stable*, 15.	In *Area*, 13. *Puteus*, 14. *Stabulum*, 15.

;and a *Bath*, 16.	cum *Balneo*, 16.
Under the House	Sub Domo
is the *Cellar*, 17.	est *Cella*, 17.

LXXIII.
The Stove with the Bed-room.

Hypocaustum cum Dormitorio.

The *Stove*, 1.	*Hypocaustum*, 1.
is beautified	ornatur
with an *Arched Roof*, 2.	*Laqueari*, 2.
:and *wainscoted Walls*, 3.	& *tabulatis Parietibus*, 3,
It is enlightened	Illuminatur
with *Windows*, 4.	*Fenestris*, 4.
It is heated	Calefit
with an *Oven*, 5.	*Fornace*, 5.
Its Utensils are	Ejus Utensilia sunt
Benches, 6.	*Scamna*, 6.
Stools, 7.	*Sellæ*, 7.
Tables, 8.	*Mensæ*, 8.
with *Tressels*, 9.	cum *Fulcris*, 9.
Footstools, 10.	ac *Scabellis*, 10.
:and *Cushions*, 11.	& *Culcitris*, 11.

There are also *Tapestries* hanged, 12.

For soft lodging
in a *Sleeping-room*, 13.
there is a *Bed*, 14.
spread on a *Bed-sted*, 15.
upon a *Straw-pad*, 16.
with *Sheets*, 17.
and *Cover-lids*, 18.

The *Bolster*, 19.
is under ones head.

The Bed is covered
with a *Canopy*, 20.

A *Chamber-pot*, 21.
is for making water in.

Appenduntur etiam
Tapetes, 12.

Pro levi cubatu,
in *Dormitorio*, 13.
est *Lectus*, (Cubile) 14.
stratus in *Sponda*, 15.
super *Stramentum*, 16.
cum *Lodicibus*, 17.
& *Stragulis*, 18.

Cervical, 19.
est sub capite.

Canopeo, 20.
Lectus tegitur.

Matula, 21.
est vesicæ levandæ.

Wells.   LXXIV.   Putei.

Where *Springs* are wanting, *Wells*, 1. are digged.
and they are compassed
about with a *Brandrith*, 2.
lest any one fall in.

Thence is water drawn

Ubi *Fontes* deficiunt,
Putei, 1. effodiuntur,
& circumdantur
Crepidine, 2.
ne quis incidat.

Inde aqua hauritur

with *Buckets*, 3.	*Urnis* (situlis), 3.
hanging either at a *Pole*, 4.	pendentibus vel *Pertica*, 4.
or a *Rope*, 5.	vel *Fune*, 5.
or a *Chain*, 6.	vel *Catena*, 6.
and that either by a *Swipe*,	idque aut *Tollenone*, 7.
7. or a *Windle*, 8.	aut *Girgillo*, 8.
or a *Turn*, 9.	aut *Cylindro*, 9.
with a *Handle*	*Manubriato.*
or a *Wheel*, 10.	aut *Rota* (tympano), 10.
or to conclude,	aut deinque
by a *Pump*, 11.	*Antliâ*, 11.

The Bath.	LXXV.	Balneum.

He that desireth to be wash'd in cold water, goeth down into a *River*, 1.	Qui cupit lavari aquâ frigidâ, descendit in *Fluvium*, 1.
In a *Bathing-house*, 2. we wash off the *filth* either sitting in a *Tub*, 3. or going up into the *Hot-house*, 4.	In *Balneario*, 2. abluimus *squalores*, sive sedentes in *Labro*, 3. sive conscendentes in *Sudatorium*, 4.

and we are rubbed with a *Pumice-stone*, 6. or a *Hair-cloth*, 5.	& defricamur *Pumice*, 6. aut *Cilicio*, 5.
In the *Stripping-room*, 7. we put off our clothes, and are tyed about with an *Apron*, 8.	In *Apodyterio*, 7. exuimus Vestes, & præcingimur *Castula* (Subligari), 8.
We cover our Head with a *Cap*, 9. and put our feet into a *Bason*, 10.	Tegimus caput *Pileolo*, 9. & imponimus pedes *Telluvio*, 10.
The *Bath-woman*, 11. reacheth water in a *Bucket*, 12. drawn out of the *Trough*, 13. into which it runneth out of *Pipes*, 14.	*Balneatrix*, 11. ministrat aquam *Situla*, 12. haustam ex *Alveo*, 13. in quem defluit è *Canalibus*, 14.
The *Bath-keeper*, 15. lanceth with a *Lancet*, 16. and by applying *Cupping-glasses*, 17. he draweth the *Blood* betwixt the skin and the flesh, which he wipeth away with a *Spunge*, 18.	*Balneator*, 15. scarificat *Scalpro*, 16. & applicando *Cucurbitas*, 17. extrahit *Sanguinem* subcutaneum, quem abstergit *Spongiâ*, 18.

The Barbers Shop.　　　LXXVI.　　　Tonstrina.

The *Barber*, 1.	*Tonsor*, 1.
in the *Barbers-shop*, 2.	in *Tonstrina*, 2.
cutteth off the *Hair*	tondet *Crines*
and the *Beard*	& *Barbam*
with a pair of *Sizzars*, 3.	*Forcipe*, 3.
or shaveth with a *Razor*,	vel radit *Novaculâ*,
which he taketh	quam depromit
out of his *Case*, 4.	è *Theca*, 4.
And he washeth one	Et lavat
over a *Bason*, 5.	super *Pelvim*, 5.
with *Suds* running	*Lixivio* defluente
out of a *Laver*, 6.	è *Gulturnio*, 6.
and also with *Sope*, 7.	ut & *Sapone*, 7.
and wipeth him	& tergit
with a *Towel*, 8.	*Linteo*, 8.
combeth him with a *Comb*,	pectit *Pectine*, 9.
9. and curleth him	crispat
with a *Crisping Iron*, 10.	*Calamistro*, 10.
Sometimes he cutteth a	Interdum secat Venam
Vein with a *Pen-knife*, 11.	*Scalpello*, 11.
where the Blood spirteth	ubi Sanguis propullulat,
out, 12.	12.

| The *Chirurgeon* cureth *Wounds*. | *Chirurgus* curat *Vulnera*. |

| The Stable. | LXXVII. | Equile. |

The *Horse-keeper*, 1. cleaneth the *Stable* from *Dung*, 2.	*Stabularias* (Equiso), 1. purgat *Stabulum* a *Fimo*, 2.
He tyeth a *Horse*, 3. with a *Halter*, 4. to the *Manger*, 5. or if he apt to bite, he maketh him fast with a *Muzzle*, 6.	Alligat *Equum*, 3. *Capistro*, 4. ad *Præsepe*, 5. aut si mordax constringit *Fiscella*, 6.
Then he streweth *Litter*, 7. under him.	Deinde substernit *Stramenta*, 7.
He *winnoweth Oats* with a *Van*, 8. (being mixt with Chaff, and taken out of a *Chest*, 10.) and with them feedeth the Horse, as also with *Hay*, 9.	*Ventilat Avenam, Vanno*, 8. (Paleis mixtam, ac depromptam à *Cista Pabulatoria*, 10.) câque pascit equum, ut & *Fœno*, 9.

Afterwards he leadeth	Postea ducit
him to the *Watering-trough*,	ad *Aquarium*, 11.
11. to water.	aquatum.
Then he rubbeth him	Tum detergit
with a *Cloth*, 12.	*Panno*, 12.
combeth him	depectit
with a *Curry-comb*, 15.	*Strigili*, 15.
covereth him	insternit
with an *Housing-cloth*, 14.	*Gausape*, 14.
and looketh upon his *Hoofs*	& inspicit *Soleas*,
whether the *Shoes*, 13.	an *Calcei ferrei*, 13.
be fast with the *Nails*.	firmis *Clavis* hæreant.

Dials.	LXXVII.	Horologia.

A *Dial*	*Horologium*
measureth Hours.	dimetitur Horas.
A *Sun-dial*, 1.	*Solarium*, 1.
sheweth by the shadow	ostendit umbrâ
of the *Pin*, 2.	*Gnomonis*, 2.
what a *Clock* it is;	quota sit *Hora* ;
either on a Wall,	sive in Pariete,
or a *Compass*, 3,	sive in *Pyxide Magnetica*, 3.
An *Hour-glass*, 4.	*Clepsydra*, 4.

sheweth the four parts of an hour by the running of *Sand*, heretofore of water. | ostendit partes horæ quatuor, fluxu *Arenæ,* olim aquæ.

A *Clock.* 5. numbereth also the Hours of the Night, by the turning of the Wheels, the greatest whereof is drawn by a *Weight*, 6. and draweth the rest. | *Automaton,* 5. numerat etiam Nocturnas Horas, circulatione Rotarum, quarum maxima trahitur à *Pondere*, 6. & trahit cæteras.

Then either the *Bell*, 7. by its sound, being struck on by the *Hammer*, or the *Hand*, 8. without, by its motion about sheweth the hour. | Tum vel *Campana*, 7. sonitu suo, percussâ a *Malleolo*, vel *Index* extra Circuitione sua indicat horam.

The Picture. LXXIX, Pictura.

Pictures, 1. delight the Eyes and adorn Rooms. | *Picturæ,* 1. oblectant Oculos & ornant Conclavia.

The *Painter*, 2. painteth an *Image* | *Pictor*, 2. pingit *Effigiem*

with a *Pencil*, 3.	*Penicilio*, 3.
in a *Table*, 4.	in *Tabula*, 4.
upon a *Case-frame*, 5.	super *Pluteo*, 5.
holding his *Pollet*, 6. in his	tenens *Orbem Pictorium*, 6.
left hand,	in sinistra,
on which are the *Paints*	in quo *Pigmenta*
which were ground by the	quæ terebantur à
Boy, 7. on a *Marble*.	*puero*, 7. in *marmore*.
The *Carver*	*Sculptor*,
and *Statuary*	& *Statuarius*
carve *Statues*, 8.	exsculpunt *Statuas*, 8.
of Wood and Stone.	è Ligno & Lapide.
The *Graver*	*Cœlator*
and the *Cutter*	& *Scalptor*
grave *Shapes*, 10.	insculpit *Figuras*, 10.
and *Characters*	& *Characteres*,
with a *Graving Chesil*, 9.	*Cœlo*, 9.
in Wood, Brass,	Ligno, Æri,
and other Metals.	aliisque Metallis.

Looking-glasses.   LXXX.   Specularia.

Looking-glasses, 1. | *Specularia*, 1.

I

are provided that Men may see themselves.	parantur, ut homines intueantur seipsos.
Spectacles, 2.	*Perspicilla*, 2.
that he may see better, who hath a weak sight.	ut cernat acius qui habet visum debilem.
Things afar off are seen in a *Perspective Glass*, 3. as things near at hand.	Remota videntur per *telescopium*, 3. ut proxima.
A *Flea* appeareth in a *muliplying-glass*, 4. like a little hog.	*Pulex*, 4. in *Microscopio* apparet ut porcellus.
The Rays of the Sun, burn wood through a *Burning-glass*, 5.	Radii Solis accendunt ligna per *Vitrum urens*, 5.

The Cooper.	LXXXI.	Vietor.

The *Cooper*, 1. having an *Apron*, 2, tied about him, maketh *Hoops* of *Hazel-rods*, 3. upon a *cutting-block*, 4. with a *Spoke-Shave*, 5.	*Vietor*, 1. amictus *Præcinctorio*, 2. facit *Circulos*, è *Virgis Colurnis*, 3. super *Sellam incisoriam*, 4. *Scalpro bimanubriato*, 5.

and *Lags*, 6. of *Timber*,	& *Assulas*, 6. ex *Ligno*.
Of *Lags* he maketh *Hogs-heads*, 7. and *Pipes*, 8.	Ex Assulis conficit *Dolia*, 7. & *Cupas*, 8.
with two *Heads ;*	*Fundo* bino;
and *Tubs*, 9.	tum *Lacus*, 9.
Soes, 10.	*Labra*, 10.
Flaskets, 11.	*Pitynas* [Trimodia], 11.
Buckets, 12.	& *Situlas*, 12.
with one Bottom.	fundo uno.
Then he bindeth them	Postea vincit
with *Hoops*, 13.	*Circulis*, 13.
which he tyeth fast	quos ligat
with small *Twigs*, 15.	*Viminibus*, 15.
by means of a *Cramp-iron*,	ope *Falcis vietoriæ*, 14.
14. and he fitteth them on	& aptat
with a *Mallet*, 16.	*Tudite*, 16.
and a *Driver*, 17.	ac *Tudicula*, 17.

LXXXII.
The Roper, and the Cordwainer.

Restio, & Lorarius.

The *Roper*, 1.	*Restio*, 1.

twisteth *Cords*, 2.	contorquet *Funes*, 2.
of *Tow*, or *Hemp*, 4.	è *Stupa*, 4. vel *Cannabi*,
(which he wrappeth about	quam circumdat
himself) by	sibi
the turning of a *Wheel*, 3.	agitatione *Rotulæ*, 3.
Thus are made	Sic fiunt,
first *Cords*, 5.	primò *Funiculi*, 5.
then *Ropes*, 6.	tum *Restes*, 6.
and at last, *Cables*, 7.	tandem *Rudentes*, 7.
The *Cord-wainer*, 8.	*Lᴏrarius*, 8.
cutteth great *Thongs*, 10.	scindit *Loramenta*, 10.
Bridles, 11.	*Fræna*, 11.
Girdles, 12.	*Cingula*, 12.
Sword-belts, 13.	*Baltheos*, 13.
Pouches, 14.	*Crumenas*, 14.
Port-mantles, 15. &c.	*Hippoperas*, 15., &c.
out of a *Beast-hide*, 9.	de *corio bubulo*, 9.

The Traveller.	LXXXIII.	Viator.

A *Traveller*, 1.	*Viator*, 1.
beareth on his shoulders	portat humeris

in a *Budget*, 2.	in *Bulga*, 2.
those things	quæ non capit
which his *Satchel*, 3.	*Funda*, 3.
or *Pouch*, 4. cannot hold.	vel *Marsupium*, 4.
He is covered	Tegitur
with a *Cloak*, 5.	*Lacernâ*, 5.
He holdeth a *Staff*, 6. in	Tenet *Baculum*, 6. **Manu**
his hand wherewith	quo
to bear up himself.	se fulciat.
He hath need of	Opus habet
Provision for the way,	*Viatico*,
as also of a pleasant and	ut & fido & facundo
merry *Companion*, 7.	*Comite*, 7.
Let him not forsake the	Non deserat *Viam*
High-road, 9. for a *Foot-*	*regiam* propter *Semitam*, 8.
way, 8. unless it be a	nisi sit
beaten Path.	*Callis tritus.*
By-ways, 10.	*Avia*, 10.
and *places where two ways*	& *Bivia*, 11.
meet, 11.	
deceive and lead men aside	fallunt & seducunt,
into *uneven-places*, 12.	in *Salebras*, 12.
so do not *By-paths*, 13.	non æquè *Tramites*, 13.
and *Cross-ways*, 14.	& *Compita*, 14.
Let him therefore en-	Sciscitet igitur
quire of *those he meeteth*,	*obvios*, 15.
15. which way he must go;	quà sit eundum;
and let him take heed	& caveat
of *Robbers*, 16.	*Prædones*, 16.
as in the *way*, so also	ut in *viâ*, sic etiam
in the *Inn*, 17. where	in *Diversorio*, 17.
he lodgeth all Night.	ubi pernoctat.

The Horse-man.   LXXXIV.   Eques.

The *Horse-man*, 1.	*Eques*, 1.

The *Horse-man*, 1.
setteth a *Saddle*, 2.
on his *Horse*, 3.
and girdeth it on
with a *Girth*, 4.

    He layeth a *Saddle-cloth*,
5. also upon him.

    He decketh him with
Trappings, a *Fore-stall*, 6.
a *Breast-cloth*, 7.
and a *Crupper*, 8.

    Then he getteth upon
his Horse, putteth his feet
into the *Stirrops*, 9. taketh the *Bridle-rein*, 10. 11.
in his left hand, wherewith
he guideth and holdeth
the Horse.

    Then he putteth to
his *Spurs*, 12.

    Eques, 1.
imponit *Equo*, 2.
Ephippium, 3.
idque succingit
Cingulo, 4.

    Insternit etiam *Dorsuale*,
5.

    Ornat eum
Phaleris, *Frontali*, 6.
Antilena, 7.
& *Postilena*, 8.

    Deinde insilit in
Equum, indit pedes
Stapedibus, 9.
capessit *Lorum* (habe-
nam),10. *Freni*, 11. sinistrâ
quo flectit, & retinet
Equum.

    Tum admovet
Calcaria, 12.

and setteth him on with a *Switch*, 13.	incitatque *Virgula*, 13.
and holdeth him in with a *Musrol*, 14.	& coërcet *Postomide*, 14.
The *Holsters*, 15.	*Bulgæ*, 15.
hang down from the *Pummel* of the *Saddle*, 16.	pendent ex *Apice Ephippii*, 16.
in which the *Pistols*, 17. are put.	quibus *Sclopi*, 17. inseruntur.
The Rider is clad in a short *Coat*, 18.	Ipse Eques induitur *Chlamyde*, 18.
his *Cloak* being tyed behind him, 19.	*Lacernâ* revinctâ, 19. à tergo.
A *Post*, 20.	*Veredarius*, 20.
is carried on Horseback at full Gallop.	fertur Equo cursim.

Carriages.	LXXXV	Vehicula.

We are carried on a *Sled*, 1. over Snow and Ice.	Vehimur *Trahâ*, 1. super Nivibus & Glacie.
A Carriage with one Wheel, is called a *Wheelbarrow*, 2.	Vehiculum unirotum, dicitur *Pabo*, 2.

with two Wheels, a *Cart*, 3.
with four Wheels, a *Wagon*,
which is either
a *Timber-wagon*, 4.
or a *Load-wagon*, 5.

The parts of the Wagon
are, the *Neep* (or draught-
tree), 6. the *Beam*, 7.
the *Bottom*, 8.
and the *Sides*, 9.

Then the *Axle-trees*, 10.
about which the *Wheels*
run, the *Lin-pins*, 11.
and *Axletree-staves*, 12. being fastened before them.

The *Nave*, 13. is the
groundfast of the *Wheel*,
14. from which come
twelve *Spokes*, 15.

The *Ring* encompasseth
these, which is made
of six *Felloes*, 16.
and as many *Strakes*, 17.
Hampiers and *Hurdles*, 18.
are set in a Wagon.

birotum, *Carrus*, 3.
quadrirotum, *Currus*,
qui vel
Sarracum, 4.
vel *Plaustrum*, 5.

Partes Currûs sunt,
Temo, 6.
Jugum, 7.
Compages, 8.
Spondæ, 9.

Tum *Axes*, 10.
circa quos *Rotæ* currunt,
Paxillis, 11.
& *Obicibus*, 12.
præfixis.

Modiolus, 13. est
Basis *Rotæ*, 14.
ex quo prodeunt
duodecim *Radii*, 15.

Orbile ambit hos,
compositum
è sex *Absidibus*, 16.
& totidem *Canthis*, 17.
Corbes & *Crates*, 18.
imponuntur Currui.

LXXXVI.

Carrying to and fro.   Vectura.

The *Coach-man*, 1.	*Auriga*, 1.
joineth a *Horse fit to match*	jungit *Parippum*, 2. *Sella-*
a *Saddle-horse*, 2, 3.	*rio*, 3.
to the *Coach-tree*,	ad *Temonem*,
with *Thongs* or *Chains*, 5.	*Loris* vel *Catenis*, 5.
hanging down from the	dependentibus
Collar, 4.	de *Helcio*, 4.
Then he sitteth upon	Deinde insidet
the *Saddle-horse*,	*Sellario*,
and driveth them that go	agit ante se antecessores, 6.
before him, 6.	
with a *Whip*, 7.	*Scuticâ*, 7.
and guideth them	& flectit
with a *String*, 8	*Funibus*, 8.
He greaseth the *Axle-tree*	Ungit *Axem*
with *Axle-tree grease*	*Axungiâ*,
out of a *Grease-pot*, 9.	ex *vase unguentorio*, 9.
and stoppeth the wheel	& inhibet rotam
with a *Trigen*, 10.	Sufflamine, 10.

in a steep descent.

And thus the Coach is driven along the *Wheel-ruts*, 11.

Great Persons are carried *with six Horses*, 12. by two *Coachmen*, in a Hanging-wagon, which is called a *Coach*, 13.

Others *with two Horses*, 14. in a *Chariot*, 15.

Horse Liiters, 16, 17. are carried by two Horses.

They use *Pack-Horses*, instead of *Waggons*, thorow *Hills* that are not passable, 18.

in præcipiti descensu.

Et sic aurigatur per *Orbitas*, 11.

Magnates vehuntur *Sejugibus*, 12. duobus *Rhedariis*, Curru pensili, qui vocatur *Carpentum* (Pilentum), 13.

Alii *Bijugibus*, 14. *Essedo*, 15.

Arceræ, 16. & *Lacticæ*, 17. portantur à duobus Equis.

Utuntur *Jumentis Clitellariis*, loco *Curruum*, per *montes* invios, 18.

LXXXVII.

Passing over Waters.   Transitus Aquarum

Lest he that is to pass over a River should be wet,

Trajecturus flumen ne madefiat,

Bridges, 1.	*Pontes*, 1.
were invented for Car-	excogitati sunt pro Ve-
riages, and *Foot-bridges*, 2.	hiculis & *Ponticuli*, 2.
for Foot-men.	pro Peditibus.
If a river	Si Flumen
have a *Foord*, 3.	habet *Vadum*, 3.
it *is waded over*, 4.	*vadatur*, 4.
Flotes, 5. also are made of	*Rates*, 5. etiam struuntur
Timber pinned together;	ex compactis tignis :
or *Ferry-boats*, 6.	vel *Pontones*, 6.
of planks laid close to-	ex trabibus consolidatis,
gether for fear they should	ne excipiant aquam.
receive Water.	
Besides *Scullers*, 7.	Porrò *Lintres* (Lembi), 7.
are made, which are rowed	fabricantur, qui
with an *Oar*, 8.	aguntur *Remo*, 8.
or *Pole*, 9.	vel *Conto*, 9.
or haled	aut trahuntur
with an *Haling-rope*, 10.	*Remulco*, 10.

Swimming.	LXXXVIII.	Natatus.

Men are wont also	Solent etiam
to swim over Waters	tranare aquas

upon a *bundle of flags*, 1. | super *scirpeum fascem*, 1.
and besides upon blown | porrò super inflatas *boum*
Beast-bladders, 2. | *Vesicas*, 2.
and after, by throwing | deinde liberè jactatu
their *Hands* and *Feet*, 3. | *Manuum Pedumque*, 3.
abroad. |

   And at last they learned | Tandem didicerunt
to tread the water, 4. | *calcare aquam*, 4.
being plunged up to the | immersi
girdle-stead, and carrying | cingulo tenus & gestantes
their *Cloaths* upon their | Vestes supra caput.
head. |

   A *Diver*, 5. | *Urinator*, 5.
can swim also under | etiam natare potest
the water like a Fish. | sub aquâ, ut Piscis.

A Galley.   LXXXIX.   Navis actuaria.

A *Ship* furnished | *Navis* instructa
with *Oars*, 1. | *Remis*, 1.
is a *Barge*, 2. | est *Uniremis*, 2.
or a *Foyst*, &c. | vel *Biremis*, &c.
in which the *Rowers*, 3. | in quâ *Remiges*, 3.

sitting on *Seats*, 4.	considentes pre *Transtra*,
by the *Oar-rings*,	4. ad *Scalmos*,
row, by striking the water	remigant pellendo aquam
with the *Oars*, 5.	*Remis*,
The *Ship-master*, 6.	*Proreta*, 6.
standing in the *Fore-castle*,	stans in *Prora*,
and the *Steers-man*, 7.	& *Gubernator*, 7.
sitting at the *Stern*,	sedens in *Puppi*,
and holding the *Rudder*, 8.	tenensque *Clavum*, 8.
steer the *Vessel*.	gubernant *Navigium*.

A Merchant-ship.   XC.   Navis oneraria.

A *Ship*, 1.	*Navigium*, 1.
is driven onward	impellitur,
not by Oars, but by the	non remis, sed
only force of the Winds.	solâ vi Ventorum.
In it is a *Mast*, 2. set up,	In illo *Malus*, 2. erigi-
fastened with *Shrowds*, 3.	tur, firmatus *Funibus*, 3.
on all sides to the *main-*	undique ad *Oras Navis*,
chains.	

to which the *Sail-yards*, 4. are tied, and the *Sails*,5. to these, which are *spread open*, 6. to the wind, and are hoysed by *Bowlings*, 7.

The Sails are
the *Main-sail*, 8.
the *Trinket*, or *Fore-sail*, 9.
the *Misen-sail* or *Poop-sail*, 10.

The *Beak*, 11.
is in the *Fore-deck*.

The *Ancient*, 12.
is placed in the *Stern*.

On the Mast
is the *Foretop*, 13.
the *Watch-tower* of the Ship and over the *Fore-top*
a *Vane*, 14.
to shew which way the Wind standeth.

The ship is stayed with an *Anchor*, 15.

The depth is fathomed with a *Plummet*, 16.

Passengers walk up and down the *Decks*, 17.

The Sea men run to and fro through the *Hatches*,18.

And thus, even Seas are passed over.

cui annectuntur *Antennæ*,4. his, *Vela*, 5. quæ *expanduntur*, 6. ad Ventum & *Versoriis*, 7. versantur.

Vela sunt
Artemon, 8.
Dolon, 9.
& *Epidromus*, 10.

Rostrum, 11.
est in *Prora*.

Signum (vexillum), 12.
ponitur in *Puppi*.

In Malo
est *Corbis*, 13.
Specula Navis
& supra *Galeam*
Aplustre, 14.
Ventorum Index.

Navis sistitur
Anchorâ, 15.

Profunditas exploratur
Bolide, 16.

Navigantes deambulant
in *Tabulato*, 17.

Nautæ cursitant
per *Foros*, 18.

Atque ita, etiam **Maria** trajiciuntur.

Ship-wreck. XCI. Naufragium.

When a *Storm*, 1. ariseth on a sudden, they strike *Sail*, 2. lest the Ship should be dashed against *Rocks*, 3 or light upon *Shelves*, 4.	Cum *Procella*, 1. oritur repentè contrahunt *Vela*, 2. ne Navis ad *Scopulos*, 3. allidatur, aut incidat in *Brevia* (Syrtes), 4.
If they cannot hinder her they suffer *Ship-wreck*, 5.	Si non possunt prohibere patiuntur *Naufragium*, 5.
And then the men, the *Wares*, and all things are miserably lost.	Tum Homines, *Merces*, omnia miserabiliter pereunt.
Nor doth the *Sheat-anchor*, 6. being cast with a *Cable*, do any good.	Neque hic *Sacra anchora*, 6. *Rudenti* jacta quidquam adjuvat.
Some escape, either on a *Plank*, 7. and by swimming, or in the *Boat*, 8.	Quidam evadunt, vel *tabula*, 7. ac enatando, vel *Scapha*, 8.
Part of the Wares, with the dead folks, is carried out of the *Sea*, 9. oupn the Shoars.	Pars Mercium cum mortuis a *Mari*, 9. in littora defertur.

Writing.   XCII.   Ars Scriptoria.

The Ancients writ
in *Tables done over with wax*
with a brazen *Poitrel*, 1.
with the *sharp end*, 2.
whereof letters were en-
graven and rubbed out
again with the *broad end*, 3.

Afterwards
they writ *Letters*
with a *small Reed*, 4.

We use a *Goose-quill*, 5.
the *Stem*, 6.
of which we make
with a *Pen-knife*, 7.
then we dip the *Neb*
in an *Ink-horn*, 8.
which is stopped
with a *Stopple*, 9.
and we put our *Pens*,
into a *Pennar*, 10.

We dry a Writing

Veteres scribebant
in *Tabellis ceratis*
æneo *Stilo*, 1.
cujus *parte cuspidata*, 2.
exarabantur literæ,
rursum vero obliteraban-
tur *planâ*.

Deinde
Literas pingebant
subtili Calamo, 4.

Nos utimur *Anserina Pen-
na*, 5. cujus *Caulem*, 6.
temperamus
Scalpello, 7.
tum intingimus *Crenam*
in *Atramentario*, 8.
quod obstruitur
Operculo, 9.
& *Pennas* recondimus
in *Calamario*, 10.

Siccamus Scripturam

with *Blotting-paper*, or *Calis-sand* out of a *Sand-box*, 11.	*Chartâ bibulâ*, vel *Arenâ scriptoria*, ex *Theca Pulveraria*, 11.
And we indeed write from the left hand towards the right, 12. the *Hebrews* from the right hand towards the left, 13. the *Chinese* and other *Indians*, from the top downwards, 14.	Et nos quidem scribimus â sinistra dextrorsum, 12. *Hebræi* â dextrâ sinistrorsum, 13. *Chinenses* & *Indi* alii, â summo deorsum, 14.

Paper.	XCIII.	Papyrus.

The Ancients used *Beech-Boards*, 1. or *Leaves*, 2. as also *Barks*, 3. of *Trees ;* especially of an Egyptian Shrub, which was called *Papyrus*.	Veteres utebantur *Tabulis Faginis*, 1. aut *Foliis*, 2. ut & *Libris*, 3. *Arborum ;* præsertim Arbusculæ Ægyptiæ, cui nomen erat *Papyrus*.
Now *Paper* is in use which the *Paper-maker*	Nunc *Charta* est in usu, quam *Chattopœus*

J

maketh in a *Paper-mill*, 4. | in *mola Papyracea*, 4. confic-
of *Linen rags*, 5. | it è *Linteis vetustis*, 5.
stamped to *Mash*, 6. | in *Pulmentum* contusis, 6.
which being taken up in | quod haustum
Frames, 7. | *Normulis*, 7.
he spreadeth into *Sheets*, 8. | diducit in *Plagulas*, 8.
and setteth them in the Air | exponitque aëri,
that they may be dryed. | ut siccentur.

    Twenty-five of these | Harum XXV.
make a *Quire*, 9. | faciunt *Scapum*, 9.
twenty Quires a *Ream*, 10. | XX. Scapi *Volumen minus*,
and ten of these | 10. horum X.
a *Bale of Paper*, 11. | *Volumen majus*, 11.

    That which is to last | Duraturum diu
long is written on *Parch-* | scribitur in *Mem-*
ment, 12. | *brana*, 12.

Printing.   XCIV.   Typographia.

    The *Printer* hath | *Typographus* habet
metal Letters | *Typos* Metallos,
in a large number | magno numero dis-
put into *Boxes*, 5. | tributos per *Loculamenta*, 5.

    The *Compositor*, 1. | *Typotheta*, 1.

taketh them out one by one	eximit illos singulatim,
and according to the *Copy*,	& secundum *exemplar*,
(which he hath fastened	(quod habet præfixum
before him in a *Visorum*, 2.)	sibi *Retinaculo*, 2.)
composeth words	componit Verba
in a *Composing-stick*, 3.	*Gnomone*, 3.
till a *Line* be made;	donec *versus* fiat;
he putteth these in a *Gally*,	hos indit *Formæ*, 4.
4. till a *Page,* 6. be made,	donec *Pagina*, 6. fiat;
and these again in a *Form*,	has iterum *Tabulâ compos-*
7. and he locketh them up	*itoriâ*, 7. coarctaque eos
in *Iron Chases*, 8.	*Marginibus ferreis*, 8.
with *Coyns*, 9.	ope *Cochlearum*, 9.
lest they should drop out,	ne dilabantur,
and putteth them under	ac subjicit
the *Press*, 10.	*Prelo*, 10.
Then the *Press-man*	Tum *Impressor*
beateth it over	illinit
with *Printers Ink*,	*Atramento impressorio*
by means of *Balls*, 11.	ope *Pilarum*, 11.
spreadeth upon it the Pa-	super imponit Chartas
pers put in the *Frisket*, 12.	inditas *Operculo*, 12.
which being put	quas subditas
under the *Spindle*, 14.	*Trochleæ*, 14.
on the *Coffin*, 13.	in *Tigello*, 13.
and pressed down with a	& impressas
Bar, 15. he maketh	*Suculâ*, 15. facit
to take impression.	imbibere typos.

XCV.

The Booksellers Shop.   Bibliopolium.

The *Bookseller*, 1
selleth *Books*
in a *Booksellers Shop*, 2.
of which he writeth
a *Catalogue*, 3.

The Books are placed
on *Shelves*, 4.
and are laid open for use
upon a *Desk*, 5.

A Multitude of Books
is called a *Library*, 6.

Bibliopola, 1.
vendit *Libros*
in *Bibliopolio*, 2.
quorum conscribit
Catalogum, 3.

Libri disponuntur
per *Repositoria*, 4.
& exponuntur ad usum,
super *Pluteum*, 5.

Multitudo Librorum
vocatur *Bibliotheca*, 6.

The Book-binder. XCVI. Biblio**pegus**.

In times past they glewed Paper to Paper, and rolled them up together into one *Roll*, 1.	Olim agglutinabant Chartam Chartæ, convolvebantque eas in unum *Volumen*, 1.

In times past they
glewed Paper to Paper,
and rolled them up to-
gether into one *Roll*, 1.

At this day
the *Book-binder*
bindeth Books,
whilst he wipeth, 2. over
Papers steept in *Gum-wa-
ter*, and then foldeth them
together, 3.
beatheth with a hammer, 4.
then stitcheth them up, 5.
presseth them in a *Press*,6.
which hath two *Screws*, 7.
glueth them on the back,
cutteth off the edges
with a *round Knife*, 8.
and at last covereth them
with *Parchment* or *Leather*,
9. maketh them handsome,
and setteth on *Clasps*, 10.

Olim agglutinabant
Chartam Chartæ,
convolvebantque eas
in unum *Volumen*, 1.

Hodiè
Compactor
compingit Libros,
dum tergit, 2.
chartas maceratas *aquâ
glutinosâ*, deinde
complicat, 3.
malleat, 4.
tum consuit, 5.
conprimit *Prelo*, 6.
quod habet duos *Cochleas*,7.
conglutinat dorso,
demarginat
rotundo *Cultro*, 8.
tandem vestit
Membranâ vel *Corio*, 9.
efformat,
& affigit *Uncinulos*, 10.

A Book. XCVII. Liber.

A *Book*	*Liber*,
as to its outward shape,	quoad exteriorem formam,
is either in *Folio*, 1.	est vel in *Folia*, 1.
or in *Quarto*, 2.	vel in *Quarto*, 2.
in *Octavo*, 3.	in *Octavo*, 3.
in *Duodecimo*, 4. either	in *Duodecimo*, 4.
made to open Side-wise, 5.	vel *Columnatus*, 5.
or *Long-wise*, 6.	vel *Linguatus*, 6.
with *Brazen Clasps*, 7.	cum *Æneis Clausuris*, 7.
or *Strings*, 8.	vel *Ligulis*, 8.
and *Square-bofles*, 9.	& *angularibus Bullis*, 9.
Within are *Leaves*, 10.	Intùs sunt *Folia*, 10.
with two *Pages*,	duabis *Paginis*,
sometimes divided with	aliquando *Columnis*, 11. di-
Columns, 11.	visa cumq;
and *Marginal Notes*, 12.	*Notis Marginalibus*, 12.

A School.　　　　XCVIII.　　　　Schola.

A *School*, 1.
is a Shop in which
Young Wits are fashion'd
to vertue, and it is
distinguish'd into *Forms*.

The *Master*, 2.
sitteth in a *Chair*, 3.
the *Scholars*, 4.
in *Forms*, 5.
he teacheth, they learn.

Some things
are writ down before them
with *Chalk* on a *Table*, 6.

Some sit
at a Table, and write, 7.
he mendeth their Faults, 8.

Some stand and rehearse
things committed to
memory, 9.

Some talk together, 10.
and behave themselves
wantonly and carelessly;

Schola, 1.
est Officina, in quâ
Novelli Animi formantur
ad virtutem, &
distinguitur in *Classes*.

Præceptor, 2.
sedet in *Cathedra*, 3.
Discipuli, 4.
in *Subselliis*, 5.
ille docet, hi discunt.

Quædam
præscribuntur illis
Cretâ in *Tabella*, 6.

Quidam sedent
ad Mensam, & scribunt, 7.
ipse corrigit Mendas, 8.

Quidam stant, & reci-
tant mandata
memoriæ, 9.

Quidam confabulantur,
10. ac gerunt se
petulantes, & negligentes;

these are chastised with a *Ferrula*. 11. and a *Rod*, 12.	hi castigantur *Ferulâ* (baculo), 11. & *Virgâ*, 12.

The Study.	XCIX.	Museum.

The *Study*, 1.	*Museum*, 1.
is a place where a Student, 2. apart from Men, sitteth alone, addicted to his *Studies*, whilst he readeth *Books*, 3. which being within his reach he layeth open upon a *Desk*, 4. and picketh all the best things out of them into his own *Manual*, 5. or marketh them in them with a *Dash*, 6. or a *little Star*, 7. in the *Margent*.	est locus ubi Studiosus, 2. secretus ab Hominibus,' sedet solus deditus *Studiis*, dum lectitat *Libros*, 3. quos penes se & exponit super *Pluteum*, 4. & excerpit optima quæque ex illis in *Manuale* suum, 5. notat in illis *Liturâ*, 6. vel *Asterisco*, 7. ad *Margiem*.
Being to sit up late,	Lucubraturus,

he setteth a *Candle*, 8. on a *Candlestick*, 9. which is snuffed with *Snuffers*, 10. before the Candle, he placeth a *Screen*, 11. which is green, that it may not hurt his eye-sight ; richer Persons use a *Taper*, for a *Tallow-candle* stinketh and smoaketh.

A *Letter*, 12. is wrapped up, writ upon, 13. and sealed, 14.

Going abroad by night, he maketh use of a *Lanthorn*, 15. or a *Torch*, 16.

elevat *Lychnum* (*Canelam*), 8. in *Candelabra*, 9. qui emungitur *Emunctorio*, 10. ante Lynchum collocat *Umbraculum*, 11. quod viride est, ne hebetet oculorum aciem ; opulentiores utuntur *Cereo* nam *Candela sebacea* fœtet & fugimat.

Epistola, 12. complicatur, inscribitur, 13. & obsignatur, 14.

Prodiens noctu utitur *Lanterna*, 15. vel *Face*, 16.

C.
Arts belonging to Speech.

Artes Sermones.

Grammar, 1. | *Grammatica*, 1.

is conversant about *Letters*, 2. of which it maketh *Words*, 3. and teacheth how to utter, write, 4. put together and part them rightly.

    Rhetorick, 5.
doth as it were paint, 6.
a rude form, 7.
of Speech with *Oratory Flourishes*, 8.
such as are *Figures*,
Elegancies,
Adagies,
Apothegms,
Sentences,
Similies,
Hierogylphicks, &c.

    Poetry, 9.
gathereth these *Flowers of Speech*, 10.

and tieth them as it were into a little *Garland*, 11.
and so making of *Prose*
a *Poem*,
it maketh several sorts of *Verses* and *Odes*,
and is therefore crowned with a *Laurel*, 12.

    Musick, 13.
setteth *Tunes*, 14.
with *pricks*,
to which it setteth words,
and so singeth alone,
or in *Consort*,
or by Voice, or
Musical Instruments, 15.

versatur circa *Literas*, 2. ex quibus componit *Voces,* *verba*, 3. docetque eloqui, scribere, 4. construere, distinguere (interpungere) eas recte.

    Rhetorica, 5.
pingit, 6. quasi
rudem *formam*, 7.
Sermonis *Oratoriis*
Pigmentis, 8.
ut sunt *Figuræ*,
Elegantiæ,
Adagia (proverbia)
Apothegmata,
Sententiæ (Gnomæ)
Similia,
Hieroglyphica, &c.

    Poesis, 9.
colligit hos *Flores Orationis*, 10.

& colligat quasi
in *Corallam*, 11.
atque ita, faciens è *prosa ligatam orationem*,
componi varia
Carmina & *Hymnos* (*Odas*)
ac propterea coronatur
Lauru, 12.

    Musica, 13.
componit *Melodias*, 14.
Notis,
quibus aptat verba,
atque ita cantat sola
vel *Concentu* (*Symphonia*),
aut voce aut
Instrumentis Musicis, 15.

Musical Instruments.   CI.   Instrumenta musica.

Musical Instruments are	Musica instrumenta sunt
those which make a sound:	quæ edunt vocem :
First,	Primò,
when they are beaten upon,	cum pulsantur,
as a *Cymbal*, 1. with a *Pestil*,	ut *Cymbalum*, 1. *Pistillo*,
a *little Bell*, 2.	*Tintinnabulum*, 2.
with an *Iron pellet* within ;	intus *Globulo ferreo*,
or *Rattle*, 3.	*Crepitaculum*, 3.
by tossing it about :	circumversando ;
a *Jews-Trump*, 4.	*Crembalum*, 4.
being put to the mouth,	ori admotum,
with the fingers ;	Digito ;
a *Drum*, 5.	*Tympanum*, 5.
and a *Kettle*, 6.	& *Ahenum*, 6.
with a *Drum-stick*, 7.	*Claviculâ*, 7.
as also the *Dulcimer*, 8.	ut & *Sambuca*, 8.
with the *Shepherds-harp*, 9.	cum *Organo pastoritio*, 9.
and the *Tymbrel*, 10.	& *Sistrum* (Crotalum), 10.
Secondly,	Secundò,
upon which *strings* are	in quibus *Chordæ*
stretched, and struck upon,	intenduntur & plectuntur
as the *Psaltery*, 11.	ut *Nablium*, 11.

and the *Virginals*, 12. | cum *Clavircordio*, 12.
with both hands; | utrâque manu;
the *Lute*, 13. | *Testudo* (Chelys), 13.
(in which is the *Neck*, 14. | (in quâ *Jugum*, 14.
the *Belly*, 15, | *Magadium*, 15.
the *Pegs*, 16. | & *Verticilli*, 16.
by which the *Strings*, 17. | quibus *Nervi*, 17.
are stretched | intenduntur
upon the *Bridge*, 18.) | super *Ponticulam*, 18.)
the *Cittern*, 19. | & *Cythara*, 19.
with the right hand only, | Dexterâ tantum,
the *Vial*, 20. | *Pandura*, 20.
with a *Bow*, 21. | *Plectro*, 21.
and the *Harp*, 23. | & *Lyra*, 23.
with a Wheel within, | intus rotâ,
which is turned about: | quæ versatur:
the *Stops*, 22. | *Dimensiones*, 22.
in every one are touched | in singulis tanguntur
with the left hand. | sinistra.

    At last, | Tandem
those which are blown, | quæ inflantur,
as with the mouth, | ut Ore,
the *Flute*, 24. | *Fistula* (*Tibia*), 24.
the *Shawm*, 25. | *Gingras*, 25.
the *Bag-pipe*, 26. | *Tibia utricularis*, 26.
the *Cornet*, 27. | *Lituus*, 27.
the *Trumpet*, 28, 29. | *Tuba*, 28. *Buccina*, 29.
or with *Bellows*, | vel *Follibus*, ut
as a *pair of Organs*, 30. | *Organum pneumaticum*, 30.

Philosophy.   CII.   Philosophia.

The *Naturalist*, 1.	*Physicus*, 1.
vieweth all the works of	speculatur omnia Dei
God in the World.	Opera in Mundo.

The *Naturalist*, 1.
vieweth all the works of
God in the World.

The *Supernaturalist*, 2.
searches out the *Causes*
and *Effects* of things.

The *Arithmetician*,
reckoneth *numbers*,
by adding, subtracting,
multiplying and dividing;
and that either by *Cyphers*,
3. on a *Slate*,
or by *Counters*, 4.
upon a *Desk*.

Country *people* reckon, 5.
with *figures of tens*, X.
and *figures of five*, V.
by *twelves, fifteens*,
and *threescores*.

Physicus, 1.
speculatur omnia Dei
Opera in Mundo.

Metaphysicus, 2.
perscrutatur *Causas*,
& rerum *Effecta*.

Arithmeticus
computat *numeros*,
addendo, subtrahendo,
multiplicando, dividendo;
idque vel *Cyphris*, 3.
in *Palimocesto*,
vel *Calculis*, 4.
super *Abacum*.

Rustici numerant, 5.
Decussibus, X.
& *Quincuncibus*, V.
per *Duodenas, Quindenas*,
& *Sexagenas*.

Geometry.   CIII.   Geometria.

A *Geometrician*
measureth the *height* of
a *Tower*, 1 . . . . 2.
or the *distance*
of *places*, 3 . . . . 4.
either with a *Quadrant*, 5.
or a *Jacob's-staff*, 6.

   He maketh out the
Figures of things,
with *Lines*, 7.
Angles, 8.
and *Circles*, 9.
by a *Rule*, 10.
a *Square*, 11.
and a *pair of Compasses*, 12.

   Out of these arise
an *Oval*, 13.
a *Triangle*, 14.
a *Quadrangle*, 15.
and other figures.

Geometra
metitur *Altitudinem*
Turris, 1 . . . . 2.
aut *distantiam*
Locorum, 3 . . . . 4.
sive *Quadrante*, 5.
sive *Radio*, 6.

   Designat
Figuras rerum
Lineis, 7,
Angulis, 8.
& *Circulis*, 9.
ad *Regulam*, 10.
Normam. 11.
& *Circinum*, 12.

   Ex his oriuntur
Cylindrus, 13.
Trigonus 14.
Tetragonus, 15.
& aliæ figuræ.

The Celestial Sphere.   CIV.   Sphera cælestis.

Astronomy considereth
the motion of the Stars,
Astrology
the Effects of them.

The Globe of Heaven
is turned about upon an
Axle-tree, 1.
about the Globe of the
Earth, 2. in the
space of XXIV. hours.

The Pole-stars, or Pole,
the Arctick, 3.
the Antarctick, 4.
conclude the Axle-tree
at both ends.

The Heaven is full of
Stars every where.

There are reckoned above
a thousand fixed Stars ;
but of Constellations
towards the North, XXI.
towards the South, XVI.

Astronomia considerat
motus Astrorum,
Astrologia
eorum Effectus.

Globus Cœli
volvitur
super Axem, 1.
circa globum
terræ, 2.
spacio XXIV. horarum.

Stellæ polares,
Arcticus, 3.
Antarcticus, 4.
finiunt Axem
utrinque.

Cœlum est
Stellatum undique.

Stellarum fixarum
numerantur plus mille ;
Siderum verò
Septentrionarium, XXI.
Meridionalium, XVI.

Add to these the XII. *signs* of the *Zodiaque*, 5. every one XXX. degrees, whose names are ♈ *Aries* ♉ *Taurus*, ♊ *Gemini*, ♋ *Cancer*, ♌ *Leo*, ♍ *Virgo*, ♎ *Libra*, ♏ *Scorpius*, ♐ *Sagittarius*, ♑ *Capricor*, ♒ *Aquarius*, ♓ *Pisces*.

Under this move the seven *Wandring-stars* which they call *Planets*, whose way is a circle in the middle of the Zodiack, called the *Ecliptick*, 6.

Other Circles are the *Horizon*, 7. the *Meridian*, 8. the *Æquator*, 9. the two *Colures*, the one of the *Equinocts*, 10. (of the *Spring* when the ☉ entreth into ♈; *Autumnal* when it entreth in ♎) the other of the *Solstices*,11. (*of the Summer*, when the ☉ entreth into ♋ of the *Winter* when it entreth into ♑) the *Tropicks*, the *Tropick of Cancer*, 12. the *Tropick of Capricorn*,13. and the two *Polar Circles*, 14....15.

Adde *Signa*, XII. *Zodiaci*, 5. quodlibet graduum, XXX. quorum nomina sunt ♈ *Aries*, ♉ *Taurus*, ♊ *Gem.* ♋ *Cancer*, ♌ *Leo*, ♍ *Virgo*, ♐ *Libra*, ♏ *Scorpius*, ♎ *Sagittarius*, ♑ *Capricorn*, ♒ *Aquarius*, ♓ *Pisces*.

Sub hoc cursitant *Stellæ errantes* VII. quas vocant *Planetas*, quorum via est Circulvs, in medio Zodiaci, dictus *Ecliptica*, 6.

Alii Circuli sunt *Horizon*, 7. *Meridianus*, 8. *Equator*, 9. duo *Coluri*, alter *Æquinoxiorum*, 10. (*Verni*, quando ☉ ingreditur ♈; *Autumnalis*, quando ingreditur ♎) alter *Solsticiorum*, 11. (*Æstivi*, quando ☉ ingreditur ♋; *Hyberni*, quando ingreditur ♑) duo *Tropici*, *Tr. Cancri*, 12. *Tr. Capricorni*, 13. & duo *Polares*, 14....15.

CIV.

The Aspects of the Planets.

Planetarum Aspectus.

The *Moon*	*Luna*
runneth through the *Zodi-ack* every *Month*.	percurrit *Zodiacum* singulis *Mensibus*.
The *Sun*, ☉ in a Year.	*Sol*, ☉ Anno.
Mercury, ☿ and *Venus*, ♀ about the Sun, the one in a hundred and fifteen, the other in 585 days.	*Mercurius*, ☿ & *Venus*, ♀ circa Solem, illa CXV., hæc DLXXXV. Diebus.
Mars, ♂ in two years;	*Mars*, ♂ Biennio;
Jupiter, ♃ in almost twelve;	*Jupiter*, ♃ ferè duodecim;
Saturn, ♄ in thirty years.	*Saturnus*, ♄ triginta annis.
Hereupon they meet variously among themselves, and have mutual Aspects one towards another.	Hinc conveniunt variè inter se & se mutuo adspiciunt.

K

As here the ☉ and ☿ are in *Conjunction*.	Ut hic sunt, ☉ & ☿ in *Conjunctione*,
☉ and *Moon* in *Opposition*,	☉ and *Luna* in *Oppositione*,
☉ and ♄ in a *Trine Aspect*,	☉ & ♄ in *Trigono*,
☉ and ♃ in a *Quartile*,	☉ & ♃ in *Quadratura*,
☉ and ♂ in a *Sextile*.	☉ & ♂ in *Sextili*.

CV.
The Apparitions of the Moon.

Phases Lunæ.

The *Moon* shineth not by her own *Light* but that which is borrowed of the *Sun*.	*Luna*, lucet non sua propria *Luce*, sed mutuatâ a *Sole*.
For the one half of it is always enlightned, the other remaineth darkish.	Nam altera ejus medietas semper illuminatur, altera manet caliginosa.
Hereupon we see it in *Conjunction* with the *Sun*, 1. to be obscure, almost none at all; in *Opposition*, 5.	Hinc videmus, in *Conjunctione Solis*, 1. obscuram, imo nullam : in *Oppositione*, 5.

whole and clear,	totam & lucidam,
(and we call it	(& vocamus
the *Full Moon ;*)	*Plenilunium ;*)
sometimes in the half,	alias dimidiam,
(and we call it the *Prime*, 3.	(& dicimus *Primam*, **3**.
and *last Quarter*, 7.)	& *ultimam Quadram*, 7.)
Otherwise it waxeth, 2..4.	Cæteroqui crescit, **2..4.**
or waneth, 6. . . 8.	aut decrescit, 6....8.
and is said to be *horned*,	& vocatur *falcata*,
or more than half *round*.	vel *gibbosa*.

The Eclipses.	CVI.	Eclipses.

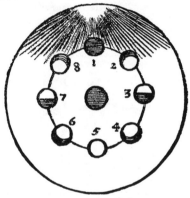

The *Sun*	*Sol*
is the fountain of light,	est fons Lucis,
inlightning all things,	illuminans omnia;
but the *Earth*, 1.	sed *Terra*, 1.
and the *Moon*, 2.	& *Luna*, 2.
being shady bodies, are not	Corpora opaca, non
pierced with its rays, for	penetrantur ejus radiis,
they cast a shadow upon	nam jaciunt umbram
the place just over against	in locum oppositum.
them.	
Therefore,	Ideo
when the Moon lighteth	cum Luna incidit

into the shadow of the *Earth*, 2. it is darkened, which we call an *Eclipse*, or defect.

in umbram *Terræ*, 2. obscuratur quod vocamus *Eclipsin* (deliquium) *Lunæ*.

But when the *Moon* runneth betwixt the *Sun* and the *Earth*, 3. it covereth it with its shadow; and this we call the *Eclipse* of the *Sun*, because it taketh from us the sight of the *Sun*, and its light; neither doth the *Sun* for all that suffer any thing, but the *Earth*.

Cum vero *Luna* currit inter *Solem* & *Terram*, 3. obtegit illum umbrâ suâ; & hoc vocamus *Eclipsin Solis*, quia adimit nobis prospectum *Solis*, & lucem ejus; nec tamen *Sol* patitur aliquid, sed *Terra*.

CVII. *a*
The terrestial Sphere.

Sphera terrestris.

The *Earth* is round, and therefore to be represented by two *Hemispheres*, a..b. The Circuit of it

Terra est rotunda, fingenda igitur duobus *Hemispheriis*, a..b. Ambitus ejus

is 360 *degrees* (whereof every one maketh 60 *English* Miles or 21600 Miles,) and yet it is but a prick, compared with the World, whereof it is the *Centre*.	est *graduum* CCCLX. (quorum quisque facit LX. Milliaria *Anglica* vel 21600 Milliarium) & tamen est punctum, collata cum orbe, cujus *Centrum* est.
They measure Longitude of it by *Climates*, 1. and the *Latitude* by *Parallels*, 2.	Longitudinem ejus dimetiuntur *Climatibus*, 1. *Latitudinem*, lineis *Parallelis*, 2.
The *Ocean*, 3. compasseth it about, and five *Seas* wash it, the *Mediterranean Sea*, 4. the *Baltick Sea*, 5. the *Red Sea*, 6. the *Persian Sea*, 7. and the *Caspian Sea*, 8.	*Oceanus*, 3. ambit eam & *Maria* V. perfundunt *Mediterraneum*, 4. *Balticum*, 5. *Erythræum*, 6. *Persicum*, 7. *Caspium*, 8.

CVII. *b*

The terrestial Sphere.

Sphera terrestris.

It is divided into V. *Zones*, whereof the II. *frigid ones*, 9....9.	Distribuitur in *Zonas* V., quarum duæ *frigidæ*, 9....9.

are uninhabitable ;
the II. *Temperate* ones, 10
..10. and the *Torrid* one,
11. habitable.

Besides it is divided
into three *Continents*;
this of ours, 12. which is
subdivided into *Europe*,13.
Asia, 14. *Africa*, 15.
America, 16..1.16.
(whose Inhabitants are
Antipodes to us;)
and the *South Land*, 17..17.
yet unknown.

They that dwell under the
North pole,18. have the days
and nights 6 months long.

Infinite *Islands*
float in the Seas.

sunt inhabitabiles ;
duæ *Temperatæ*, 10....10.
& *Torrida*, 11.
habitantur.

Ceterum divisa est
in tres *Continentes ;*
nostram, 12. quæ subdi-
viditur in *Europam*, 13.
Asiam, 14. & *Africam*, 15.
in *Americam*, 16....16.
(cujus incolæ
sunt *Antipodes* nobis;)
& in *Terram Australem*, 17
..17. adhuc incognitam.

Habitantes sub *Arcto*,
18. habent Dies
Noctes semestrales,

Infinitæ *Insulæ*
natant in maribus.

Europe.   CVIII.   Europa.

The chief *Kingdoms* of
Europe, are

In *Europâ* nostrâ
sunt *Regna* primaria,

Spain, 1.	*Hispania*, 1.
France, 2.	*Gallia*, 2.
Italy, 3.	*Italia*, 3.
England, 4.	*Anglia* (Britania), 4.
Scotland, 5.	*Scotia*, 5.
Ireland, 6.	*Hibernia*, 6.
Germany, 7.	*Germania*, 7.
Bohemia, 8.	*Bohemia*, 8.
Hungary, 9.	*Hungaria*, 9.
Croatia, 10.	*Croatia*, 10.
Dacia, 11.	*Dacia*, 11.
Sclavonia, 12.	*Sclavonia*, 12.
Greece, 13.	*Græcia*, 13.
Thrace, 14.	*Thracia*, 14.
Podolia, 15.	*Podolia*, 15.
Tartary, 16.	*Tartaria*, 16.
Lituania, 17.	*Lituania*, 17.
Poland, 18.	*Polonia*, 18.
The *Netherlands*, 19.	*Belgium*, 19.
Denmark, 20.	*Dania*, 20.
Norway, 21.	*Norvegia*, 21.
Swethland, 22.	*Suecia*, 22.
Lapland, 23.	*Lappia*, 23.
Finland, 24.	*Finnia*, 24.
Lisland, 25.	*Livonia*, 25.
Prussia, 26.	*Borussia*, 26.
Muscovy, 27.	*Muscovia*, 27.
and *Russia*, 28.	*Russia*, 28.

Moral Philosophy. CIX. Ethica.

⟨⟩ This *Life* is a *way*,	*Vita* hæc est *via*,
or a *place divided into two ways*, like	sive *Bivium*, simile
Pythagoras's Letter Y.	Litteræ *Pithagoricæ* Y.
broad, 1.	latum, 1.
on the left hand track;	sinistro tramite
narrow, 2. on the right;	angustum, 2. dextro;
that belongs to *Vice*, 3.	ille *Vitii*, 3. est
this to *Vertue*, 4.	hic *Virtutis*, 4.
Mind, Young Man, 5.	Adverte juvenis, 5.
imitate *Hercules*:	imitare *Herculem;*
leave the left hand way,	linque sinistram,
turn from Vice;	aversare Vitium;
the *Entrance*, 6. is fair,	*Aditus* speciosus, 6.
but the *End*, 7.	sed *Exitus*, 7.
is ugly and steep down.	turpis & præceps.
Go on the right hand,	Dextera ingredere,
though it be thorny, 8.	utut spinosa, 8.
no way is unpassible to	nulla via invia
vertue; follow whither	virtuti; sequere quâ viâ
vertue leadeth	ducit virtus

through *narrow places* to *stately palaces*, to the *Tower of honour*, 9. | per *angusta*, ad *augusta*, ad *Arcem honoris*, 9.

Keep the middle and streight *path*, and thou shalt go very safe. | Tene medium & rectum *tramitem;* ibis tutissimus.

Take heed thou do not go too much on the right hand, 10. | Cave excedas ad dextram, 10.

Bridle in, 12. the wild Horse, 11. of Affection, lest thou fall down headlong. | Compesce freno, 12. equum ferocem, 11. Affectûs ne præceps fias.

See thou dost not go amiss on the left hand, 13. in an ass-like sluggishness, 14. but go onwards constantly, persevere to the end, and thou shalt be crown'd, 15. | Cave deficias ad sinistram, 13. segnitie asininâ, 14. sed progredere constanter pertende ad finem, & coronaberis, 15.

Prudence.   CX.   Prudentia.

Prudence, 1. looketh upon all things | *Prudentia*, 1. circumspectat omnia

as a *Serpent*, 2.
and doeth, speaketh, or
thinketh nothing in vain.

  She *looks backwards*, 3.
as into a *Looking-glass*, 4.
to *things past ;*
and seeth *before her*, 5.
as with a *Perspective-glass*,
7. *things to come,*
or the *End*, 6.
and so she perceiveth
what she hath done, and
what remaineth to be done.

  She proposeth
an *Honest, Profitable* and
withal, if it may be done,
a *Pleasant End*,
to her Actions.

  Having foreseen the *End*,
she looketh out *Means*,
as a *Way*, 8.
which leadeth to the End;
but such as are certain
and easie, and fewer
rather than more, lest
anything should hinder.

  She watcheth *Opportuni-
ty*, 9. (which having
a *bushy fore-head*, 10.
and being *bald-pated*, 11.
and moreover
having wings, 12.
doth quickly slip away,)
and catcheth it.

  She goeth on her way
warily, for fear she should
stumble or go amiss.

ut *Serpens*, 2.
agitque, loquitur, aut
cogitat nihil incassum.

  Respicit, 3.
tanquam in *Speculum*, 4.
ad *præterita ;*
& *prospicit*, 5.
tanquam *Telescopio*, 7.
Futura,
seu *Finem*, 6.
atque ita perspicit
quid egerit,
& quid restet agendum.

  Actionibus suis
præfigit *Scopum*,
Honestum, Utilem,
simulque, si fieri potest,
Jucundum.

  Fine prospecto,
dispicit *Media*,
ceu *Viam*, 8.
quæ ducit ad finem,
sed certa & facilia ;
pauciora potiùs
quàm plura,
ne quid impediat.

  Attendit *Occasioni*, 9.
(quæ
Fronte Capillata, 10.
sed vertice *calva*, 11.
adhæc
alata, 12.
facile elabitur)
eamque captat.

  In viâ pergit cautè (pro-
vidè) ne impingat
aut aberret.

Diligence.   CXI.   Sedulitas.

Diligence, 1. loveth labours, avoideth *Sloth*, is always at work, like the *Pismire*, 2. and carrieth together, as she doth, for herself, *Store* of all things, 3.

She doth not always sleep, or make holidays, as the *Sluggard*, 4. and the *Grashopper*, 5. do, whom *Want*, 6. at the last overtaketh.

She pursueth what things she hath undertaken chearfully, even to the end; she putteth nothing off till the morrow, nor doth she sing the *Crow's* song, 7. which saith over and over,

Sedulitas, 1. amat labores, fugit *Ignaviam*, semper est in *opere*, ut *Formica*, 2. & comportat, ut illa, sibi, omnium rerum *Copiam*, 3.

Non semper dormit, ferias agit, aut ut *Ignavus*, 4. & *Cicada*, 5. quos *Inopia*, 6. tandem premit.

Urget incepta alacriter ad finem usque; procrastinat nihil, nec cantat cantilenam *Corvi*, 7. qui ingeminat

Cras, Cras.

After *labours undergone,*
and ended,
being even wearied,
she resteth her self;
but being refreshed with
Rest, that she may not use
her self to *Idleness,* she fall-
eth again to her *Business,*

A diligent *Scholar*
is like *Bees,* 8.
which carry honéy
from divers *Flowers,* 9.
into their *Hive,* 10.

Cras, Cras,

Post *labores*
exantlatos,
& lassata,
quiescit;
sed recreata *Quiete,*
ne adsuescat
Otio, redit
ad *Negotia.*

Diligens *Discipulus,*
similis est *Apibus,* 8.
qui congerunt mel
ex variis *Floribus,* 9.
in *Alveare* suum, 10.

Temperance.   CXII.   Temperantia.

Temperance, 1.
prescribeth a mean
to *meat* and *drink,* 2.
and restraineth the *desire,*
as with a *Bridle,* 3.

Temperantia, 1.
præscribit *modum*
Cibo & *Potui,* 2.
& continet *cupidinem,*
ceu *Freno,* 3.

and so moderateth all things, lest any thing too much be done.	& sic moderatur omnia ne quid nimis fiat.
Revellers are made *drunk*, 4. they *stumble*, 5. they *spue*, 6. and *babble*, 7.	*Heluones* (ganeones) *inebriantur*, 4. *titubant*, 5. *ructant* (vomunt), 6. & *rixantur*, 7.
From *Drunkenness* proceedeth *Lasciviousness ;* from this a *lewd Life* amongst *Whoremasters*, 8. and *Whores*, 9. in *kissing*, *touching*, *embracing*, and *dancing*, 10.	E *Crapula* oritur *Lascivia;* ex hâc *Vita libidinosa* inter *Fornicatores*, 8. & *Scorta*, 9. *osculando* (basiando), *palpando*, *amplexando*, & *tripudiando*, 10.

Fortitude.	CXIII.	Fortitudo.

Fortitude, 1. is undaunted in adversity,	*Fortitudo*, 1. impavida est in adversis,

and bold as a *Lion*, 2. but not haughty in Prosperity, leaning on her own *Pillar*, 3. *Constancy*, and being the same in all things, ready to undergo both *estates* with an even mind.	& confidens ut *Leo*, 2. at non tumida in Secundis, innixa suo *Columini*, 3. *Constantiæ ;* & eadem in omnibus, parata ad ferendam utramque *fortunam* æquo animo.
She receiveth the strokes of *Misfortune* with the *Shield*, 4. of *Sufferance :* and keepeth off the *Passions*, the enemies of quietness with the *Sword*, 5. of *Valour*.	Excipit ictus *Infortunii Clypeo*, 4. *Tolerantiæ :* & propellit *Affectus*, hostes Euthymiæ *gladio*, 5. *Virtutis.*

Patience.	CXIV.	Patientia.

Patience, 1. endureth *Calamities*, 2.	*Patientia*, 1. tolerat *Calamitates*, 2.

and *Wrongs*, 3. meekly like a *Lamb*, 4. as the Fatherly *chastisement of God*, 5.

In the meanwhile she leaneth upon the *Anchor of Hope*, 6. (as a *Ship*, 7. tossed by waves in the Sea) *she prayeth to God*, 8. weeping, and expecteth the *Sun*, 10. after *cloudy weather*, 9. suffering evils, and hoping better things.

On the contrary, the *impatient person*, 11. waileth, lamenteth, *rageth against himself*, 12. grumbleth like a *Dog*, 13. and yet doth no good; at the last he despaireth, and becometh *his own Murtherer*, 14.

Being full of rage he desireth to revenge wrongs.

& *Injurias*, 3. humiliter ut *Agnus*, 4. tanquam paternam *ferulam Dei*, 5.

Interim innititur *Spei Anchoræ*, 6. (ut *Navis*, 7. fluctuans mari) *Deo supplicat*, 8. illacrymando, & expectat *Phœbum*, 10. post *Nubila*, 9. ferens mala, sperans meliora.

Contra, *Impatiens*, 11. plorat, lamentatur, *debacchatur*, 12. *in seipsum*, obmurmurat ut *Canis*, 13. & tamen nil proficit; tandem desperat, & fit *Autochir*, 14.

Furibundus cupit vindicare injurias.

Humanity.   CXV.   Humanitas.

Men are made	*Homines* facti sunt
for one another's *good ;*	ad mutua *commoda ;*
therefore let them be *kind.*	ergò sint *humani.*
Be thou sweet and lovely	Sis suavis & amabilis
in thy *Countenance,* 1.	*Vultu,* 1.
gentle and civil	comis & urbanus
in thy *Behaviour* and *Man-*	*Gestu* ac *Moribus,* 2.
ners, 2.	
affable and true spoken	affabilis & verax,
with thy *Mouth,* 3.	*Ore,* 3.
affectionate and *candid*	candens & *candidus*
in thy *Heart,* 4.	*Corde,* 4.
So love,	Sic ama,
and so shalt thou be loved;	sic amaberis ;
and there will be	& fiat
a mutual *Friendship,* 5.	mutua *Amicitia,* 5.
as that of *Turtle-doves,* 6.	ceu *Turturum,* 6.
hearty, gentle, and	concors, mansueta,
wishing well on both parts.	& benevola utrinque.
Froward Men are	Morosi homines, sunt
hateful, teasty, unpleasant.	odiosi, torvi, illepidi.

contentious, *angry,* 7.	contentiosi, *iracundi,* 7.
cruel, 8.	*crudeles,* 8.
and implacable,	ac implacabiles,
(rather Wolves and Lions,	(magis Lupi & Leones,
than Men)	quàm homines)
and such as fall out among	& inter se discordes,
themselves, hereupon	hinc
they fight in a *Duel,* 9.	confligunt *Duelle,* 9.
Envy, 10.	*Invidia,* 10.
wishing ill to others,	malè cupiendo aliis,
pineth away her self.	conficit seipsam.

Justice.	CXVI.	Justitia.

Justice, 1.	*Justitia,* 1.
is painted, sitting	pingitur, sedens
on a *square stone,* 2. for she	in *lapide quadrato,* 2. nam
ought to be immoveable;	decet esse immobilis;
with *hood-winked eyes,* 3.	*obvelatis oculis,* 3.
that she may not respect	ad non respiciendum
persons;	personas;
stopping the left ear, 4.	*claudens aurem sinistram,* 4.

L

to be reserved
for the other party;
   Holding in her right
Hand a *Sword*, 5.
and a *Bridle*, 6.
to punish
and restrain evil men;
   Besides,
a pair of Balances, 7.
in the *right Scale*, 8. whereof *Deserts*,
and in the *left*, 9.
Rewards being put,
are made even one with
another, and so good Men
are incited to virtue, as it
were with *Spurs*, 10.
   In *Bargains*, 11.
let Men deal candidly,
let them stand to their
Covenants and *Promises;*
let *that which is given one
to keep*,
and *that which is lent*,
be restored:
let no man be *pillaged*, 12.
or *hurt*, 13.
let every one have his own:
these are the precepts of
Justice.
   Such things as these are
forbidden in *God's* 5*th.* and
7*th. Cammandment*, and
deservedly punish'd on the
Gallows and the *Wheel*, 14.

reservandam
alteri parti;
   Tenens dextrâ
Gladium, 5.
& *Frænum*, 6.
ad puniendum
& coërcendum malos;
   Præterea,
Stateram, 7.
cujus *dextræ Lanci*, 8.
Merita,
Sinistræ, 9.
Præmia imposita,
sibi invicem exequantur,
atque ita boni incitantur
ad virtutem,
ceu *Calcaribus*, 10.
   In *Contractibus*, 11.
candidè agatur:
stetur
Pactis & *Promissis;*
Depositum,

& *Mutuum*,
reddantur:
nemo *expiletur*, 12.
aut *lædatur*, 13.
suum cuique tribuatur:
hæc sunt præcepta
Justitiæ.
   Talio prohibentur,
quinto & *septimo Dei
Præcepto*, &
merito puniuntur
Cruce ac *Rotâ*, 14.

Liberality.   CXVII.   Liberalitas.

Liberality, 1.
keepeth a mean about
Riches, which she honestly
seeketh, that she may have
somewhat to bestow on
them that *want*, 2.

She *cloatheth*, 3.
nourisheth, 4.
and *enricheth*, 5.
these with a *chearful coun-
tenance*, 6.
and a *winged hand*, 7.

She submitteth her
wealth, 8. to her self, not
her self to it, as the *covet-
ous man*, 9. doth, who hath,
that he may have, and is
not the *Owner*,
but the *Keeper* of his goods,
and being unsatiable,
always *scrapeth together*, 10.
with his Nails.

Liberalitas, 1.
servat modum circa
Divitias, quas honestè
quærit ut habeat
quod largiatur
Egenis, 2.

Hos *vestit*, 3.
nutrit, 4.
ditat, 5.
Vultu hilari, 6.

& *Manu alatâ*, 7.

Subjicit
opes, 8. sibi, non
se illis, ut *Avarus*, 9.
qui habet,
ut habeat, &
non est *Possessor*
sed *Custos* bonorum suor-
um, & insatiabilis,
semper *corradit*, 10.
Unguibus suis.

Moreover he spareth and keepeth, *hoarding up*, 11. that he may always have.	Sed & parcit & adservat, *occludendo*, 11. ut semper habeat.
But the *Prodigal*, 12. badly spendeth things well gotten, and at the last wanteth.	At *Prodigus*, 12. malè disperdit benè parta, ac tandem eget.

CXVIII.
Society betwixt Man and Wife.

Societas Conjugalis.

Marriage was appointed by God in Paradise, for mutual *help*, and the *Propagation* of mankind.	*Matrimonium* institutum est à Deo in Paradiso, ad mutuum *adjutorium*, & *propagationem* generis humani.
A young man (*a single man*) being to be married, should be furnished either with *Wealth*, or a *Trade* and *Science*,	*Vir Juvenis* (*Cœlebs*) conjugium initurus, instructus sit aut *Opibus*, aut *Arte* & *Scientiâ*,

which may serve
for getting a living;
that he may be able
to maintain a *Family*.

Then he chooseth himself
a *Maid* that is *Marriageable*,
(or a *Widow*)
whom he loveth; never-
theless a greater Regard
is to be had of *Virtue*,
and *Honesty*,
than of *Beauty* or *Portion*.

Afterwards, he doth not
betroth her to himself
closely, but entreateth
for her as a *Woer*,
first to the *Father*, 1.
and then the *Mother*, 2.
or the *Guardians*,
or *Kinsfolks*, by such
as help to make the match, 3.

When she is espous'd to
him, he becometh the *Bride-
groom*, 4. and she the *Bride*,
5. and the *Contract* is made.
and an *Instrument* of *Dow-
ry*, 6. is written.

At the last
the *Wedding* is made,
where they are joined to-
gether by the *Priest*, 7.
giving their *Hands*, 8. one
to another.
and *Wedding-rings*, 9.
then they feast with the
witnesses that are invited.

After this they are called
Husband and *Wife;*
when she is dead he be-
cometh a *Widower*.

quæ sit
de pane lucrando; ʼ
ut possit
sustentare *Familiam*.

Deinde eligit sibi
Virginem Nubilem,
(aut *Viduam*)
quam adamat; ubi
tamen major ratio
habenda *Virtutis*
& *Honestatis,*
quàm *Formæ* aut *Dotis.*

Posthæc, non clam des-
pondet sibi eam,
sed ambit,
ut *Procus,*
apud *Patrem,* 1.
& *Matrem,* 2.
vel apud *Tutores,*
& *Cognatos,* per
Pronubos, 3.

Eâ sibi desponsâ,
fit *Sponsus,* 4.
& ipsa *Sponsa,* 5.
fiuntque *Sponsalia,*
& scribitur *Instrumentum
Dotale,* 6.

Tandem
fiunt *Nuptiæ*
ubi copulantur
à *Sacerdote,* 7.
datis *Manibus,* 8. ultrò ci-
troque,
& *Annulis Nuptialibus,* 9.
tum epulantur cum
invitatis testibus.

Abhinc dicuntur
Maritus & *Uxor;*
hâc mortuâ ille fit
Viduus.

CXIX.
The Tree of Consanguinity,

Arbor Consanguinitatis.

In *Consanguinity*	*Hominem*, 1.
there touch a *Man*, 1.	*Consanguinitate* attingunt,
in *Lineal Ascent*,	*in Linea ascendenti*,
the *Father*	*Pater*
(the *Father-in-law*), 2.	(*Vitricus*), 2.
and the *Mother*	& *Mater*
(the *Mother-in-law*), 3.	(*Noverca*), 3.
the *Grandfather*, 4.	*Avus*, 4.
and the *Grandmother*, 5.	& *Avia*, 5.
the *Great Grandfather*, 6.	*Proavus*, 6.
and the *Great Grandmother*,	& *Proavia*, 7.
7. the *great great*	
Grandfather, 8.	*Abavus*, 8.
the *great great*	
Grandmother, 9.	& *Abavia*, 9.
the *great great Grand-*	
father's Father, 10.	*Atavus*, 10.
the *great great Grand-*	
mother's Mother, 11.	& *Atavia*, 11

the *great great Grand-father's Grandfather*, 12.	*Tritavus*, 12.
the *great great Grand-mother's Grandmother*, 13.	& *Tritavia*, 13.
Those beyond these are called *Ancestors*, 14... 14.	Ulteriores dicuntur *Majores*, 14... 14.
In a *Lineal descent*, the *Son* (*the son-in-law*), 15. and the *Daughter*, (*the Daughter-in-law*), 16.	In *Linea descendenti*, *Filius* (*Privignus*), 15. & *Filia* (*Privigna*), 16.
the *Nephew*, 17.	*Nepos*, 17.
and the *Neece*, 18.	& *Neptis*, 18.
the *Nephews Son*, 19. and the *Nephews Daughter*, 20.	*Pronepos*, 19. & *Proneptis*, 26.
the *Nephews Nephew*, 21.	*Abnepos*, 21.
and the *Neeces Neece*, 22.	& *Abneptis*, 22.
the *Nephews Nephews Son*, 23.	*Atnepos*, 23.
the *Neeces Neeces Daughter*, 24.	& *Atneptis*, 24.
the *Nephews Nephews Ne-phew*, 25.	*Trinepos*, 25. & *Trineptis*, 26.
the *Neeces Neeces Neece*, 26.	Ulteriores dicuntur
Those beyond these are called *Posterity*, 27... 27.	*Posteri*, 27....27.
In a *Collateral Line* are the *Uncle by the Fathers side*, 28.	In *Linea Collaterali* sunt *Patruus*, 28.
and the *Aunt by the Fathers side*, 29.	& *Amita*, 29.
the *Uncle by the Mothers side*, 30.	*Avunculus*, 30.
and the *Aunt by the Mo-thers side*, 31.	& *Matertera*, 31.
the *Brother*, 32.	*Frater*, 32.
and the *Sister*, 33.	& *Soror*, 33.
the *Brothers Son*, 34.	*Patruelis*, 34.
the *Sisters Son*, 35.	*Sobrinus*, 35.
and the *Cousin by the Bro-ther* and *Sister*, 36.	& *Amitinus*, 36.

CXX.

The Society betwixt Parents and Children.

Societas Parentalis.

Married Persons,	*Conjuges,*
(by the blessing of God)	(ex benedictione Dei) sus-
have *Issue,*	cipiunt *Sobolem* (Prolem)
and become *Parents.*	& fiunt *Parentes.*
The *Father,* 1. begetteth	*Pater,* 1. generat
and the *Mother,* 2. beareth	& *Mater,* 2. parit
Sons, 3. and *Daughters,* 4.	*Filios,* 3. & *Filias,* 4.
(sometimes *Twins*).	(aliquando *Gemellos*).
The *Infant,* 5.	*Infans,* 5.
is wrapped in	involvitur
Swadling-cloathes, 6.	*Fasciis,* 6.
is laid in a *Cradle,* 7.	reponitur in *Cunas,* 7.
is suckled by the Mother	lactatur a matre
with her *Breasts,* 8.	*Uberibus,* 8.
and fed with *Pap,* 9.	& nutritur *Pappis,* 9.
Afterwards it learneth	Deinde discit
to go by a *Standing-stool,* 10.	incedere *Seperasto,* 10.

playeth with *Rattles*, 11.	ludit *Crepundiis*, 11.
and beginneth to speak.	& incipit fari.
As it beginneth to grow older, it is accustomed to *Piety*, 12.	Crescente ætate, adsuescit *Pietati*, 12.
and *Labour*, 13.	& *Labori*, 13.
and is chastised, 14.	& castigatur, 14.
if it be not dutiful.	si non sit morigerus.
Children owe to Parents Reverence and Service.	*Liberi* debent Parentibus Cultum & Officium.
The Father maintaineth his Children *by taking pains*, 15.	Pater sustentat Liberos, *laborando*, 15.

CXXI.

The Society betwixt Masters and Servants.

Societas herilis.

The *Master* (*the goodman of the House*), 1. hath *Men-servants*, 2.	*Herus* (*Pater familias*), 1. habet *Famulos* (*Servos*), 2.

the *Mistress*	*Hera*
(*the good wife of the House*),	(*Mater familias*), 3.
3. *Maidens*, 4.	*Ancillas*, 4.
They appoint these their	Illi mandant his
Work, 6.	*Opera*, 6.
and divide	& distribuunt
them their tasks, 5. which	*Laborum Pensa*, 5. qua
are faithfully to be done by	ab his fideliter sunt exse-
them without murmuring	quenda sine murmure
and loss: for which their	& dispendio; pro quo
Wages, and *Meat* and *Drink*	*Merces* & *Alimonia*
is allowed them.	præbentur ipsis.
A *Servant* was heretofore	*Servus* olim erat *Man-*
a *Slave*,	*cipium*, in quem Domino
over whom the Master had	potestas fuit
power of life and death.	vitæ & necis
At this day the poorer	Hodiè pauperiores
sort serve in a free man-	serviunt liberè,
ner, being hired for Wages.	conducti mercede.

A City.	CXXII.	Urbs.

Of many Houses	Ex multis Domibus
is made a *Village*, 1.	fit *Pagus*, 1.

or a *Town*, or a *City*, 2.

That and this are fenced and begirt with a *Wall*, 3. a *Trench*, 4.
Bulwarks, 5.
and *Pallisadoes*, 6.

Within the Walls is the *void Place*, 7. without, the *Ditch*, 8.

In the Walls are *Fortresses*, 9. and *Towers*, 10. *Watch-Towers*, 11. are upon the higher places.

The entrance into a City is made out of the *Suburbs*, 12. through *Gates*, 13. over the *Bridge*, 14.

The *Gate* hath a *Portcullis*, 15. a *Draw-bridge*, 16. *two-leaved Doors*, 17. *Locks* and *Bolts*, as also *Barrs*, 18.

In the Suburbs are *Gardens*, 19. and *Garden-houses*, 20. and also *Burying-places*, 21.

vel *Oppidum*, vel *Urbs*, 2.

Istud & hæc muniuntur & cinguntur *Mœnibus* (*Muro*), 3. *Vallo*, 4.
Aggeribus, 5.
& *Vallis*, 6.

Intra muros est *Pomœrium*, 7. extrà, *Fossa*, 8.

In mœnibus sunt *Propugnacula*, 9. & *Turres*, 10. *Specula*, 11. extant in editioribus locis.

Ingressus in Urbem fit ex *Suburbio*, 12. per *Portam*, 13. super *Pontem*, 14.

Porta habet *Cataractas*, 15. *Pontem versatilem*, 16. *Valvas*, 17. *Claustra* & *Repagula*, ut & *Vectes*, 18.

In Suburbiis sunt *Horti*, 19. & *Suburbana*, 20. ut & *Cœmeteria*, 21.

CXXIII.

The inward parts of a City.

Interiora Urbis.

Within the City are   Intra urbem sunt .
Streets, 1.   *Plateæ* (Vici), 1.
paved with Stones;   stratæ Lapidibus;
Market-places, 2.   *Fora*, 2.
(in some places with   (alicubi cum
Galleries), 3.   *Porticibus*), 3.
and *narrow Lanes*, 4,   & *Angiportus*, 4.

The Publick Buildings   Publica ædificia
are in the middle of the   sunt in medio Urbis,
City, the *Church*, 5.   *Templum*, 5.
the *School*, 6.   *Schola*, 6.
the *Guild-Hall*, 7.   *Curia*, 7.
the *Exchange*, 8.   *Domus Mercaturæ*, 8.

About the Walls and the   Circa Mœnia, & Portas
Gates are the *Magazine*, 9.   *Armamentarium*, 9.
the *Granary*, 10.   *Granarium*, 10.
Inns, Ale-houses,   *Diversoria, Popinæ,*
Cooks-shops, 11.   & *Cauponæ*, 11.

the *Play-house*, 12.
and the *Spittle*, 13.
  In the by-places
are *Houses of Office*, 14.
and the *Prison*, 15.
  In the chief Steeple
is the *Clock*, 16. and the
Watchmans Dwelling, 17.
  In the Streets are *Wells*, 18.
  The *River*, 19. or *Beck*, runneth about the City, serveth to wash away the *filth*.
  The *Tower*, 20. standeth in the highest part of the City.

Theatrum, 12.
Nosodochium, 13.
  In recessibus,
Foricæ (Cloacæ), 14.
& *Custodia* (Carcer), 15.
  In turre primariâ
est *Horologium*, 16.
& habitatio *Vigilum*, 17.
  In Plateis sunt *Putei*, 18.
  Fluvius, 19. vel *Rivus*, interfluens Urbem, inservit eluendis *sordibus*.
  Arx, 20. extat in summo Urbis.

| Judgment. | CXXIV. | Judicium. |

The best Law, is a quiet *agreement*, made either by themselves,

Optimum Jus, est placida *conventio*, facta vel ab ipsis,

betwixt whom the sute is, | inter quos lis est
or by an *Umpire*. | vel ab *Arbitro*.

If this do not proceed, | Hæc si non procedit,
they come into *Court*, 1. | venitur in *Forum*, 1.
(heretofore they judg'd | (olim judicabant
in the Market-place; at | in Foro,
this day in the *Moot-hall*) | hodiè in *Prætorio*)
in which the *Judge*, 2. | cui *Judex* (Prætor), 2.
sitteth with his *Assessors*,3. | præsidet cum *Assessoribus*,
the *Clerk*, 4. taketh | 3. *Dicographus*, 4. excipit
their Votes in writing. | Vota calamo.

The *Plaintiff*, 5. | *Actor*, 5.
accuseth the *Defendant*, 6. | accusat *Reum*, 6.
and produceth *Witnesses*,7. | & producit *Testes*, 7.
against him. | contra illum.

The *Defendant* excuseth | *Reus* excusat
himself by a *Counsellor*, 8. | se per *Advocatum*, 8.
whom the Plaintiff's *Coun-* | cui Actoris *Procurator*, 9.
sellor, 9. contradicts. | contradicit.

Then the *Judge* | Tum *Judex*
pronounceth *Sentence*, | *Sententiam* pronunciat,
acquitting the *innocent*, | absolvens *insontem*,
and condemning | & damnans
him that is *guilty*, | *sontem*
to a *Punishment*, | ad *Pœnam*,
or a *Fine*, | vel *Mulctam*,
or *Torment*. | vel ad *Supplicium*.

CXXV.
The Tormenting of Malefactors.

Supplicia Malefactorum.

Malefactors, 1.	*Malefici*, 1.
are brought	producuntur,
from the *Prison*, 3.	è *Carcere*, 3.
(where they are wont to be	(ubi torqueri solent)
tortured) by *Serjeants*, 2.	per *Lictores*, 2.
or *dragg'd with a Horse*, 15.	vel *Equo raptantur*, 15.
to place of *Execution*.	ad locum *Supplicii*.
Thieves, 4.	*Fures*, 4.
are hanged by the *Hang-man*, 6. on a *Gallows*, 5.	suspenduntur a *Carnifice*, 6. in *Patibulo*, 5.
Whoremasters	*Mœchi*
are beheaded, 7.	decollantur, 7.
Murtherers	*Homicidæ* (Sicarii)
and *Robbers* are	ac *Latrones* (Piratæ)
either laid upon a *Wheel*, 8.	vel imponuntur *Rotæ*
having their *Legs broken*,	*crucifragio plexi*, 8.
or fastened upon a *Stake*, 9.	vel *Palo* infiguntur, 9.
Witches	*Striges* (Lamiæ)

are burnt in a *great Fire*, 10.

Some before they are executed have their *Tongues cut out*, 11.
or have their *Hand*, 12.
cut off upon a *Block*, 13. or
are burnt with *Pincers*, 14.

They that have their Life given them,
are set on the *Pillory*, 16.
or *strapado'd*, 17. are
set upon a *wooden Horse*, 18.
have their *Ears cut off*, 19.
are *whipped with Rods*, 20.
are branded,
are banished,
are condemned
to the *Gallies*, or to
perpetual Imprisonment.

Traytors are pull'd in pieces with four *Horses*.

cremantur super *Rogum*, 10.

Quidam antequam supplicio
afficiantur *elinguantur*, 11.
aut plectuntur *Manu*, 12.
super *Cippum*, 13.
aut *Forcipibus*, 14. uruntur
Vitâ donati,

constringuntur *Numellis*, 16. luxantur, 17.
imponuntur *Equuleo*, 18.
truncantur Auribus, 19.
cæduntur Virgis, 20.
Stigmate notantur,
relegantur,
damnantur
ad *Triremes*, vel ad
Carcerem perpetuum.

Perduelles discerpuntur *Quadrigis*.

Merchandizing.   CXXVI.   Mercatura.

Wares	Merces,
brought from other places	aliunde allatæ, aliunde
are either exchanged	vel commutantur
in an *Exchange*, 1.	in *Domo Commerciorum*, 1,
or exposed to sale	vel exponuntur venum
in *Warehouses*, 2.	in *Tabernis Mercimoniorum*,
and they are sold	2. & venduntur
for *Money*, 3.	pro *Pecuniâ* (monetâ), 3.
being either measured	vel mensuratæ
with an *Eln*, 4.	*Ulnâ*, 4.
or weighed	vel ponderatæ
in a *pair of Balances*, 5.	*Librâ*, 5.
Shop-keepers, 6.	Tabernarii. 6.
Pedlars, 7.	*Circumforanei*, 7.
and *Brokers*, 8.	& *Scrutarii*, 8.
would also be called	etiam volunt dici
Merchants, 9.	*Mercatores*, 9.
The *Seller*	*Venditor*
braggeth of a thing	ostentat rem
that is to be sold,	promercalem,

M

and setteth the rate of it,	& indicat pretium,
and how much	quanti
it may be sold for.	liceat.
The *Buyer*, 10. cheapneth	*Emptor*, 10. licetur,
and offereth the price.	& pretium offert.
If any one	Si quis
bid *against him*, 11. the	*contralicetur*, 11.
thing is delivered to him	ei res addicitur
that promiseth the most.	qui pollicetur plurimum.

CXXVII.

Measures and Weights.	Mensuræ & Pondera.

We measure things that	Res continuas **metimur**
hang together with an *Eln*,	*Ulnâ*, 1.
1. liquid things	liquidas
with a *Gallon*, 2.	*Congio*, 2.
and dry things	aridas
by a *two-bushel Measure*, 3.	*Medimno*, 3.
We try the heaviness of	Gravitatem rerum **ex-**
things by *Weights*, 4.	perimur *Ponderibus*, 4.
and *Balances*, 5.	& *Librâ* (bilance), 5.
In this is first	In hâc primò est

the *Beam*, 6.	*Jugum* (Scapus), 6.
in the midst whereof is a	in cujus medio
little *Axle-tree*, 7. above	*Axiculus*, 7. superiùs
the *cheeks* and the *hole*, 8.	*trutina* & *agina*, 8.
in which the *Needle*, 9.	in quâ *Examen*, 9.
moveth it self to and fro :	sese agitat :
on both sides	utrinque
are the *Scales*, 10.	sunt *Lances*, 10.
hanging by *little Cords*, 11.	pendentes *Funiculis*, 11.
The *Brasiers balance*, 12.	*Statera*, 12.
weigheth things by hang-	ponderat res, suspendendo
ing them on a *Hook*, 13.	illas *Unco*, 13.
and the *Weight*, 14.	& *Pondus*, 14.
opposite to them which	ex opposito, quod
in (a) weigheth just as	in (a) æquiponderat
much as the thing,	rei,
in (b) twice so much	in (b) bis tantum,
in (c) thrice so much, &c.	in (c) ter, &c.

Physick   CXXVIII.   Ars Medica.

The *Patient*, 1.	*Ægrotans*, 1.
sendeth for a *Physician*, 2.	accersit *Medicum*, 2.

who feeleth his *Pulse*, 3,	qui tangit ipsius *Arteriam*,
and looketh upon his *Water*, 4. and then prescribeth	3. & inspicit *Urinam*, 4. tum præscribit *Medicamentum* in *Schedula*, 5.
a *Receipt* in a *Bill*, 5.	
That is made ready	Istud paratur
by an *Apothecary*, 6.	à *Pharmacopæo*, 6.
in a *Apothecaries Shop*, 7.	in *Pharmacopolio*, 7.
where *Drugs*	ubi *Pharmaca*
are kept in *Drawers*, 8.	adservantur in *Capsulis*, 8.
Boxes, 9.	*Pyxidibus*, 9.
and *Gally-pots*, 10.	& *Lagenis*, 10.
And it is	Estque
either a *Potion*, 11.	vel *Potio*, 11.
or *Powder*, 12.	vel *Pulvis*, 12.
or *Pills*, 13.	vel *Pillulæ*, 13.
or *Trochisks*, 14.	vel *Pastilli*, 14.
or an *Electuary*, 15.	vel *Electuarium*, 15.
Diet and *Prayer*, 16.	*Diæta* & *Oratio*, 16.
is the best *Physick*.	est optima *Medicina*.
The *Chirurgeon*, 18.	*Chirurgus*, 18.
cureth *Wounds*, 17.	curat *Vulnera*, 17.
and *Ulcers*,	& *Ulcera*,
with *Plasters*, 19.	*Spleniis* (emplastris), 19.

A Burial. CXXIX. Sepultura.

Dead Folks	*Defuncti*
heretofore were burned,	olim cremabantur,
and their Ashes	& Cineres
put into an *Urn*, 1.	recondebantur in *Urna*, 1.
We enclose	Nos includimus
our *dead Folks*	nostros *Demortuos*
in a *Coffin*, 2.	*Loculo*, (*Capulo*), 2.
lay them upon a *Bier*, 3.	imponimus *Feretro*, 3.
and see they be carried out	& curamus efferri
in a *Funeral Pomp*	*Pompâ Funebri*
towards the *Church-yard*,4.	versus *Cœmeterium*, 4.
where they are laid	ubi inferuntur,
in a *Grave*, 6.	*Sepulchro*, 6.
by the *Bearers*, 5.	a *Vespillonibus*, 5.
and are interred ;	& humantur ;
this is covered with	hoc tegitur
a *Grave-stone*, 7.	*Cippo*, 7.
and is adorned	& ornatur
with *Tombs*, 8.	*Monumentis*, 8.
and *Epitaphs*, 9.	ac *Epitaphiis*, 9.

As the Corps go along	Funere prodeunte,
Psalms are sung,	*Hymni* cantantur,
and the *Bells* are rung, 10.	& *Campanæ*, 10. pulsantur.

A Stage-play.	CXXX.	Ludus Scenicus.

In a *Play-house*, 1.	In *Theatro*, 1.
(which is trimmed	(quod vestitur
with *Hangings*, 2. and	*Tapetibus*, 2. &
covered with *Curtains*, 3.)	tegitur *Sipariis*, 3.)
Comedies and *Tragedies* are	*Comediæ* vel *Tragœdiæ*
acted,	aguntur,
wherein memorable things	quibus repræsentantur res
are represented;	memorabiles
as here, the History	ut hic, Historia
of the *Prodigal Son*, 4.	de *Filio Prodigo*, 4.
and his *Father*, 5.	& *Patre*, 5. ipsius,
by whom he is entertain'd,	à quo recipitur,
being return'd home.	domum redux.
The *Players* act	*Actores* (*Histriones*) agunt.
being in disguise;	personati;
the *Fool*, 6. maketh Jests.	*Morio*, 6. dat Jocos.

The chief of the Specta-tors sit in the *Gallery*, 7. the common sort stand on the *Ground*, 8. and clap the hands, if anything please them.	Spectatorum primarii, sedent in *Orchestra*, 7. plebs stat in *Cavea*, 8. & plaudit, si quid arridet.

Sleights.	CXXXI.	Præstigiæ.

The *Tumbler*, 1. maketh several *Shows* by the nimbleness of his body, walking to and fro on his hands, leaping through a *Hoop*, 2. &c. Sometimes also he *danceth*, 4. having on a Vizzard. The *Jugler*, 3. sheweth *sleights*, out of a *Purse*.	*Præstigiator*, 1. facit varia *Spectacula*, volubilitate corporis, deambulando *manibus*, saliendo per *Circulum*, 2. &c. Interdum etiam *tripudiat*, 4. Larvatus. *Agyrta*, 3. facit *præstigias* è *Marsupio*.

The *Rope-dancer*, 5.	*Funambulus*, 5.
goeth and danceth	graditur & saltat
upon a *Rope*,	super *Funem*,
holdeth a *Poise*, 6.	tenens *Halterem*, 6.
in his hand;	manu;
or hangeth himself	aut suspendit se
by the *hand* or *foot*, 7. &c.	*manu* vel *pede*, 7. &c.

The Fencing-School.　　CXXXII.　　Palestra.

Fencers	*Pugiles*
meet in a Duel	congrediuntur Duello
in a *Fencing-place*,	in *Palestra*,
fighting with *Swords*, 1.	decertantes vel *Gladiis*, 1.
or *Pikes*, 2.	vel *Hastilibus*, 2.
and *Halberds*, 3.	& *Bipennibus*, 3.
or *Short-swords*, 4.	vel *Semispathis*, 4.
or *Rapiers*, 5.	vel *Ensibus*, 5.
having balls at the point	*mucronem obligatis*,
(lest they wound one	(ne lædet
another mortally)	lethaliter)
or with *two edged-Swords*	vel *Frameis*
and a *Dagger*, 6. together.	& *Pugione*, 6. simul.

Wrestlers, 7.	*Luctatores*, 7.
(among the Romans	(apud Romanos
in time past were nayked	olim nudi
and anointed with Oyl)	& inuncti Oleo)
take hold of one another	prehendunt se invicem
and strive whether	& annituntur uter
can throw the other,	alterum prosternere pos-
especially by *tripping up his*	sit, præprimis
heels, 8.	*supplantando*, 8.
Hood-winked Fencers, 9.	*Andabatæ*, 9.
fought with their fists in	pugnabant pugnis
a ridiculous strife, to wit,	ridiculo certamine,
with their Eyes coverered.	nimirum Oculis obvelatis.

Tennis-play.	CXXXIII.	Ludus Pilæ.

In a *Tennis Court*, 1.	In *Sphæristerio*, 1.
they play with a *Ball*, 2.	luditur *Pilâ*, 2.
which one throweth,	quam alter mittit,
and another taketh,	alter excipit,
and sendeth it back	& remittit
with a *Racket*, 3.	*Reticulo*, 3.

and that is the Sport
of Noble Men
to stir their Body.
    A *Wind-ball*, 4.
being filled with Air,
by means of a *Ventil*,
is tossed to and fro
with the *Fist*, 5.
in the open Air.

idque est Lusus
Nobilium ad
commotionem Corporis.
    Follis (pila magna), 4.
distenta Aere
ope *Epistomii*,
reverberberatur
Pugno, 5.
sub Dio.

| Dice-play. | CXXXIV. | Ludus Aleæ. |

We play with *Dice*, 1.
either they that throw the
most *take up all*;
or we throw them
through a *Casting-box*, 2.
upon a *Board*, 3.
marked with figures,
and this is *Dice-players game*
at *casting Lots*.

    Men play by *Luck* and
Skill at *Tables*.
in a *pair of Tables*, 4.

Tesseris (*talis*), 1. ludimus vel *Plistobolindam* ;

vel immittimus illas
per *Frittillum*, 2.
in *Tabellam*, 3.
notatam numeris,
idque est *Ludas Sortilegii*
Aleatorum,

    Sorte & *Arte* luditur
Calculis
in *Alveo aleatorio*, 4.

and at *Cards*, 5.

We play at *Chesse* on a *Chesse-board*, 6. where only art beareth the sway.

The most ingenious Game is the Game of *Chesse*, 7. wherein as it were two Armies fight together in Battel.

& *Chartis lusoriis*, 5.

Ludimus *Abaculis* in *Abaco*, 6. ubi sola ars regnat.

Ingeniosissimus Ludus est Ludus *Latrunculorum*, 7. quo veluti duo Exercitus confligunt Prælio.

Races.   CXXXV.   Cursus Certamina.

Boys exercise themselves by running, either upon the *Ice*, 1. in *Scrick-shoes*, 2. where they are carried also upon *Sleds*, 3. or in the open Field, making a *Line*, 4. which he that desireth to win, ought to touch, but not to run beyond it.

Heretofore *Runners*, 5. run betwixt *Rails*, 6.

Pueri exercent se cursu, sive super *Glaciem*, 1. *Diabatris*, 2. ubi etiam vehuntur *Trahis*, 3. sive in Campo, designantes *Lineam*, 4. quam qui vincere cupit debet attingere, at non ultrâ procurrere.

Olim decurrebant *Cursores*, 5. inter *Cancellos*, 6.

to the *Goal*, 7. and	ad *Metam*, 7. &
he that toucheth it first	qui primum contingebat
receiveth the *Prize*, 8. from	eam, accipiebat *Brabeum*,
him that gave the prize, 9.	(*præmium*), 8. à *Brabeuta*, 9.
At this day *Tilting*	Hodie *Hastiludia*
(or the quintain) is used,	habentur,
(where a *Hoop*, 11.	(ubi *Circulus*, 11.
is struck at with	petitur
a *Truncheon*, 10.) in-	*Lancea*, 10.)
stead of *Horse-races*, which	loco *Equiriorum*, quæ
are grown out of use.	abierunt in desuetudinem.

Boys Sport.   CXXXVI.   Ludi Pueriles.

Boys use to play	*Pueri* solent ludere
either with *Bowling-stones*	vel *Globis fictilibus*, 1.
1. or throwing a *Bowl*, 2.	vel jactantes *Globum*, 2.
at *Nine-pins*, 3.	ad *Conas*, 3.
or striking a *Ball*,	vel mittentes *Sphærulam*
through a *Ring*, 5.	per *Annulum*, 5.
with a *Bandy*, 4.	*Clava*, 4.
or scourging a *Top*, 6.	versantes *Turbinem*, 6.
with a *Whip*, 7.	*Flagello*, 7.

or shooting with a *Trunk*,8. and a *Bow*, 9. or going upon *Stilts*, 10. or tossing and swinging themselves upon a *Merry-totter*, 11.	vel jaculantes *Sclopo*, 8. & *Arcu*, 9. vel incidentes *Grallis*, 10. vel super *Petaurum*, 11. se agitantes & oscillantes.

CXXXVII.
The Kingdom and the Region.

Regnum & Regio.

Many *Cities* and *Villages* make a *Region* and a *Kingdom*. The *King* or *Prince* resideth in the *chief City*, 1. the *Noblemen, Lords,* and *Earls* dwell in the *Castles*, 2. that lie about it; the *Country People* dwell in *Villages*, 3.	Multæ *Urbes* & *Pagi* faciunt *Regionem* & *Regnum*. *Rex* aut *Princeps* sedet in *Metropoli*. 1. *Nobiles, Barones,* & *Comites* habitant in *Arcibus*, 2. circumjacentibus; *Rustici* in *Pagis*, 3.

He hath his *toll-places*	Habet *telonia sua*
upon *navigable Rivers*, 4.	juxta *Flumina navigabilia*,
and *high-Roads*, 5.	4. & *Vias regias*, 5.
where *Portage* and *Tollage*	ubi *Portorum* & *Vectigal*
is exacted of them	exigitur
that sail	a navigantibus
or travel.	& iter facientibus.

CXXXVIII.

Regal Majesty.	Regia Majestas.

The *King*, 1.	*Rex*, 1.
sitteth on his *Throne*, 2.	sedet in suo *Solio*, 2.
in Kingly State,	in regio splendore,
with a stately *Habit*, 3.	magnifico *Habitu*, 3.
crowned with a *Diadem*, 4.	redimitus *Diademate*, 4.
holding a *Scepter*, 5.	tenens *Sceptrum*, 5.
in his Hand,	manu,
being attended with	stipatus
a Company of *Courtiers*.	frequentiâ *Aulicorum*.
The chief among these,	Inter hos primarii sunt
are the *Chancellor*, 6.	*Cancellarius*, 6.
with the *Counsellors*	cum *Consiliariis*

and *Secretaries,*	& *Secretariis,*
the *Lord-marshall,* 7.	*Præfectus Prætorii,* 7.
the *Comptroller,* 8.	*Aulæ Magister,* 8.
the *Cup-bearer,* 9.	*Pocillator* (pincerna), 9.
the *Taster,* 10.	*Dapifer,* 10.
the *Treasurer,* 11.	*Thesaurarius,* 11.
the *High Chamberlain,* 12.	*Archi-Cubicularius,* 12.
and the *Master of the Horse,* 13.	& *Stabuli Magister,* 13.
There are subordinate to these	Subordinantur his
the *Noble Courtiers,* 14.	*Nobiles Aulici,* 14.
the *Noble Pages,* 15.	*Nobile Famulitium,* 15.
with the *Chamberlains,*	cum *Cubiculariis,*
and *Lacquies,* 16.	& *Cursoribus,* 16.
the *Guard,* 17.	*Stipatores,* 17.
with their *Attendance.*	cum *Satellitio.*
He solemnly giveth Audience to the *Ambassadors* of Foreign Princes, 18.	Solemniter recipit *Legatos* exterorum, 18.
He sendeth	Ablegat
his *Vice-gerents,*	*Vicarios* suos,
Deputies,	*Administratores,*
Governors, Treasurers,	*Præfectos, Quæstores,*
and *Ambassadors*	& *Legatos,*
to other places,	aliorsum,
to whom he sendeth	quibus mittit
new Commissions ever	*Mandata nova*
and anon by the *Posts,* 19.	subinde per *Veredarios,* 19.
The *Fool,* 20.	*Morio,* 20.
maketh Laughter	movet Risum
by his toysom Actions.	ludicris Actionibus.

The Soldier. CXXXIX. Miles.

If we be to make War Soldiers are lifted, 1.	Si bellandum est scribuntur *Milites.* 1.

If we be to make War
Soldiers are lifted, 1.

Their *Arms* are
a *Head-piece,* 2.
(which is adorned with a
Crest) and the *Armour,*
whose parts are a *Collar,*3.
a *Breast-plate,* 4.
Arm-pieces, 5.
Leg-pieces, 6.
Greaves, 7.
with a *Coat of Mail,* 8.
and a *Buckler,* 9. these
are the defensive Arms.

The offensive are
a *Sword,* 10.
a *two-edged Sword,* 11.
a *Falchion,* 12.
which are put up into
a *Scabbard,* 13.
and are girded with a *Gir-
dle,* 14. or *Belt,* 15.

Si bellandum est
scribuntur *Milites.* 1.

Horum *Arma* sunt,
Galea (Cassis, 2.)
(quæ ornatur
Cristâ) & *Armatura,*
cujus partes *Torquis fer-
reus,* 3. *Thorax,* 4.
Brachialia, 5.
Ocreæ ferreæ, 6.
Manicæ, 7.
cum *Lorica,* 8.
& *Scuto* (Clypeo), 9.
hæc sunt Arma defensiva.

Offensiva sunt
Gladius, 10.
Framea, 11.
& *Acinaces,* 12.
qui reconduntur
Vaginâ, 13.
accinguntur *Cingu-
lo,* 14. vel *Baltheo,* 15.

(a *Scarf*, 16.	(*Fascia militaris*, 16.
serveth for ornament)	inservit ornatui)
a *two handed-Sword*, 17.	*Romphæa*, 17.
and a *Dagger*, 18.	& *Pugio*, 18.
In these is the *Haft*, 19.	In his est *Manubrium*,19.
with the *Pummel*, 20.	cum *Pomo*, 20.
and the *Blade*, 21.	& *Verutum*, 21.
having a *Point*, 22.	*Cuspidatum*, 22.
in the middle are the	in medio
Back, 23. and the *Edge*, 24.	*Dorsum*, 23. & *Acies*, 24.
The other Weapons are	Reliqua arma sunt
a *Pike*, 25. a *Halbert*, 26.	*Hasta*, 25. *Bipennis*, 26.
(in which is the *Haft*, 27.	(in quibus *Hastile*, 27.
and the *Head*, 28.) a	& *Mucro*, 28.)
Club,29. and a *Whirlebat*,30.	*Clava*, 29. & *Cæstus*, 30.
They fight at a distance	Pugnatur eminùs
with *Muskets*, 31.	*Bombardis* (Sclopetis), 31.
and *Pistols*, 32. which	& *Sclopis*, 32. quæ
are charged with *Bullets*,	onerantur *Globis*, 33.
33. out of a *Bullet-bag*, 34.	è *Theca bombardica*, 34.
and with *Gun-powder*	& *Pulvere nitrato*
out of a *Bandalier*, 35.	è *Pyxide pulveraria*, 35.

The Camps.	CXL.	Castra.

When a *Design* is under-taken the *Camp*, 1. is pitched and the *Tents* of *Canvas*, 2. or *Straw*, 3. are fastned with *Stakes ;* and they entrench them about for security's sake, with *Bulwarks*, 4. and *Ditches*, 5. *Sentinels*, 6. are also set ; and *Scouts*, 7. are sent out.

Sallyings out, 8. are made for Forage and Plunder-sake, where they often cope with the *Enemy*, 9. in skirmishing.

The *Pavilion* of the *Lord General* is in the midst of the *Camp*, 10.

Expeditione sus-ceptâ, *Castra*, 1. locantur & *Tentoria Lin-teis*, 2. vel *Stramentis*, 3. figuntur *Paxillis ;* eaque circumdant, securitatis gratiâ *Aggeribus*, 4. & *Fossis*, 5. *Excubiæ*, 6. constituuntur; & *Ex-ploratores*, 7. emittuntur.

Excursiones, 8. fiunt Pabulationis & Prædæ causâ, ubi sæpius confligitur cum *Hostibus*, 9. velitando.

Tentoriùm summi Imperatoris est in medio *Castrorum*, 10.

The Army and the Fight. CXLI. Acies & Prœlium.

When the *Battel* | Quando *Pugna*

is to be fought the | committenda est,
Army is set in order, and | *Acies* instruitur, &
divided into the *Front*, 1. | dividitur in *Frontem*, 1.
the *Rere*, 2. | *Tergum*, 2.
and the *Wings*, 3. | & *Alas* (*Cornua*), 3.
  The *Foot*, 4. | *Peditatus*, 4.
are intermixed | intermiscetur
with the *Horse*, 5. | *Equitatui*, 5.
  That is divided | Ille distinguitur
into *Companies*, | in *Centurias*,
this into *Troops*. | hic in *Turmas*.
  These carry *Banners*, 6. | Illæ in medio ferunt
those *Flags*, 7. | *Vexilla*, 6.
in the midst of them, | hæ *Labara*, 7.
  Their Officers are, | Eorum Præfecti sunt,
Corporals, *Ensigns*, | *Decuriones*, *Signiferi*,
Lieutenants, *Captains*, 8. | *Vicarii*, *Centuriones*, 8.
Commanders of the Horse, 9. | *Magistri Equitum*, 9.
Lieutenant Colonels, | *Tribuni*,
Colonels, | *Chiliarchæ*,
and he that is the chief of | & summus omnium
all, the *General*. | *Imperator*.
  The *Drummers*, 10. | *Tympanistæ*, 10.
and the *Drumslades*, 11. | & *Tympanotribæ*, 11.
as also the *Trumpeters*, 12. | ut & *Tubicines*, 12.
call to Arms, | vocant ad Arma
and inflame the Soldier. | & inflammant Militem.
  At the first Onset | Primo Conflictu,
the *Muskets*, 13. and | *Bombardæ*, 13. &
Ordnance, 14. are shot off. | *Tormenta*, 14. exploduntur.
  Afterwards they fight, | Postea pugnatur, 15.
15. hand to hand | cominus
with *Pikes* and *Swords*. | *Hastis* & *Gladiis*.
  They that are overcome | *Victi*
are *slain*. 16. | *trucidantur*, 16.
or taken prisoners, | vel capiuntur,
or *run away*, 17. | vel *aufugiunt*, 17.
  They that are for the Re- | *Succenturiati*, 18.
serve, 18. |
come upon them | superveniunt

out of their *places where they lay in wait*.	ex *insidiis*.
The *Carriages*, 19. are plundered.	*Impedimenta*, 19. spoliantur.

The Sea-Fight.　　CXLII.　　Pugna Navalis.

A *Sea-fight*	*Navale prœlium*
is terrible,	terribile est,
when huge *Ships*,	quum ingentes *Naves*,
like *Castles*,	veluti *Arces*,
run one upon another	concurrunt
with their *Beaks*, 1.	*Rostris*, 1.
or shatter one another	aut se invicem quassant
with their *Ordnance*, 2.	*Tormentis*, 2.
and so being bored thorow	atque ita perforatæ,
they drink in	imbibunt
their own Destruction,	perniciem suam
and are *sunk*, 3.	& *submerguntur*, 3.
Or when they are set on fire and either by the firing of *Gun-powder*, 4.	Aut quum igne corripiuntur, & vel ex incendio *pulveris tormentarii*, 4.

men are blown up into the air, or are burnt in the midst of the waters, or else leaping into the Sea are drowned.

A *Ship* that flieth away, 5. is overtaken by those that *pursue her*, 6. and is taken.

homines ejiciuntur in ærem, vel exuruntur in mediis aquis, vel etiam desilientes in mare, suffocantur.

Navis fugitiva, 5. intercipitur ab *insequentibus*, 6. & capitur.

CXLIII.

The Besieging of a City.   Obsidium Urbis.

A *City* that is like to endure a *Siege*, is first summoned by a *Trumpeter*, 1. and persuaded to *yield*.

Which if it refuseth to do, it is assaulted by the Besiegers, and taken by storm.

Either by climbing over the walls with *Scaling-ladders*, 2.

Urbs passura *Obsidionem*, primum provocatur per *Tubicinem*, 1. & invitatur ad *Depitionem*.

Quod si abnuat facere, oppugnatur ab Obsidentibus & occupatur.

Vel muros per *Scalas*, 2. transcendendo,

or breaking them down
with *Battering-engins*, 3.
or demolishing them
with *great Guns*, 4.
or breaking through the
Gates with a *Petarr*, 5.
or casting *Granadoes*, 6.
out of *Mortar-pieces*, 7.
into the City,
by *Engineers*, 8.
(who lye behind
Leaguer-baskets, 9.)
or overthrowing it with
Mines by *Pioneers*, 10.
   They that are besieged
defend themselves
from the *Walls*, 11.
with fire and stones, &c.,
or *break out by force*, 12.
   A *City*
that is taken by Storm
is plundered,
destroyed,
and sometimes laid even
with the ground.

aut diruendo
Arietibus, 3.
aut demoliendo
Tormentis, 4.
vel dirumpendo
portas *Exostra*, 5. vel
ejaculando *Globos Tormen-*
tarios, 6. e *Mortariis* (*balis-*
tis), 7. in Urbem
per *Balistarios*, 8.
(qui latitant post
Gerras, 9.)
vel subvertendo
Cuniculis per *Fossores*, 10.
   Obsessi
defendunt se
de *Muris*, 11.
ignibus, lapidibus, &c.
aut *erumpunt*, 12.
   Urbs
vi expugnata,
diriditur,
exciditur,
interdum equatur
solo.

Religion.　　　CXLIV.　　　Religio.

Godliness, 1.	*Pietas*, 1.
the Queen of Vertues,	Regina Virtutum
worshippeth God, 4. devout-	*colit Deum*, 4. humiliter,
ly, the Knowledge of God	Notitiâ Dei,
being drawn either from	haustâ vel ex
the *Book of Nature*, 2.	*Libro Naturæ*, 2.
(for the work commendeth	(nam opus commendat
the Work-master)	Artificem)
or from the	vel ex
Book of Scripture, 3.	*Libro Scripturæ*, 3.
she meditateth upon his	recolit
Commandments contained	Mandata ejus compre-
in the *Decalogue*, 5. and	hensa in *Decalogo*, 5.
treading Reason under	& conculcans Rationem,
foot, that *Barking Dog*, 6.	*oblatrantem Canem*, 6.
she giveth *Faith*, 7.	præbet *Fidem*, 7.
and assent	& assensum
to the Word of God,	Verbo Dei,
and *calleth* upon him, 8.	eumque *invocat*, 8. ut
as a Helper in adversity.	Opitulatorem in adversis.
Divine Services	*Officia Divina*

are done in the *Church*, 9.

in which are the *Quire*, 10.

with the *Altar*, 11.

the *Vestry*, 12.

the *Pulpit*, 13.

Seats, 14.

Galleries, 15.

and a *Font*, 16.

All men perceive that there is a God, but all men do not rightly know God.

Hence are divers *Religions* whereof IV. are reckoned yet as the chief.

fiunt in *Templo*, 9.

in quo est *Penetrale* (Adytum, 10.) cum *Altari*, 11.

Sacrarium, 12.

Suggestus, 13.

Subsellia, 14.

Ambones, 15.

& *Baptisterium*, 16.

Omnes homines sentiunt esse Deum, sed non omnes rectè nôrunt Deum.

Hinc diversæ *Religiones* quarum IV. numerantur adhuc primariæ.

Gentilism.   CXLV.   Gentilimus.

The *Gentiles* feigned to themselves near upon XIIM. *Deities*.

The chief of them were *Jupiter*, 1. *President*, and *petty-God of Heaven ;*

Gentiles finxerunt sibi prope XIIM. *Numina*.

Eorum præcipua erant *Jupiter*, 1. *Præses* & *Deaster cœli ;*

Neptune, 2. of the Sea;	*Neptunus*, 2. Maris;
Pluto, 3. of Hell;	*Pluto*, 3. Inferni;
Mars, 4. of War;	*Mars*, 4. Belli;
Apollo, 5. of Arts;	*Apollo*, 5. Artium ;
Mercury, 6. of Thieves,	*Mercurius*, 6. Furum,
Merchants,	Mercatorum,
and Eloquence;	& Eloquentiæ;
Vulcan, (*Mulciber*)	*Vulcanus* (*Mulciber*),
of Fire and Smiths;	Ignis & Fabrorum;
Æolus, of Winds:	*Æolus*, Ventorum ;
and the most obscene of	& obscænissimus,
all the rest, *Priapus*.	*Priapus*.

They had also Womanly Deities: such as were *Venus*, 7. the Goddess of Loves, and Pleasures, with her little son *Cupid*, 8. *Minerva* (*Pallas*), with the nine *Muses of Arts*; *Juno*, of Riches and Weddings; *Vesta*, of Chastity; *Ceres*, of Corn; *Diana*, of Hunting, and Fortune; and besides these *Morbona*, and *Febris* her self.

Habuerant etiam Muliebria Numina: qualia fuerunt *Venus*, 7. Dea Amorum, & Voluptatum, cum filiolo *Cupidine*, 8. *Minerva* (*Pallas*), cum novem *Musis Artium*; *Juno*, Divitiarum & Nuptiarum; *Vesta*, Castitatis; *Ceres*, Frumentorum; *Diana*, Venationum; & Fortuna : quin & *Morbona*, ac *Febris* ipsa.

The *Egyptians*, instead of God worshipped all sorts of Beasts and Plants, and whatsoever they saw first in the morning.

Ægyptii, pro Deo colebant omne genus Animalium & Plantarum, & quicquid conspiciebantur primum mane.

The *Philistines* offered to *Moloch*,9. their Children to be burnt alive,

Philistæi offerebant *Molocho* (*Saturno*), 9. Infantes cremandos vivos.

The *Indians*, 10. even to this day, worship the *Devil*, 11.

Indi, 10. etiamnum venerantur *Cacodæmona*, 11.

Yet the true *Worship*
of the true *God*,
remained with the *Patri-*
archs, who lived before
and after the Flood.

Amongst these,
that Seed of the Woman,
the *Messias* of the World,
was promised to *Abraham*,
1. the Founder of the *Jews*,
the Father of them that
believe: and he (being
called away from the Gen-
tiles) with his Posterity,
being marked with the *Sac-*
rament of Circumcision, 2.
made a peculiar people,
and *Church* of God.

Afterwards God
gave his *Law*, written
with his own Finger
in *Tables of Stone*, 5.
to this people

Verus tamem *Cultus*
veri *Dei*,
remansit apud *Patriarchas*,
qui vixerunt ante
& post Diluvium.

Inter hos,
Semen illud Mulieris,
Messias Mundi,
promissus est *Abrahamo*. 1.
Conditori *Judæorum*,
Patri credentium :
& ipse (avocatus
a Gentilibus)
cum Posteris,
notatus *Sacra-*
mento Circumcisionis, 2.
constitutus singularis
populus, & *Ecclesia* Dei.

Postea Deus
exhibuit *Legem* suam,
scriptam Digito suo
in *Tabulis Lapideis*, 5.
huic Populo

by *Moses*, 3. | per *Mosen*, 3.
in Mount *Sinai*, 4. | in Monte *Sinai*, 4.

Furthermore, he ordained the eating the *Paschal Lamb*, 6. and *Sacrifices* to be offered upon an *Altar*, 7. by *Priests*, 8. and *Incense*, 9. and commanded a *Tabernacle*, 10. with the Ark of the Covenant, 11. to be made: and besides, a *brazen Serpent*, 12. to be set up against the biting of Serpents in the Wilderness.

Porrò ordinavit manducationem *Agni Paschalis*, 6. & *Sacrificia* offerenda in *Altari*, 7. per *Sacerdotes*, 8. & *Suffitus*, 9. & jussit *Tabernaculum*, 10. cum Arca Fœderis, 11. fieri: præterea, *æneum Serpentem*, 12. erigi contra morsum Serpentum in Deserto.

All which things were *Types* of the *Messias* to come, whom the *Jews* yet look for.

Quæ omnia *Typi* erant *Messiæ* venturi, quem *Judæi* adhuc expectant.

Christianity.   **CXLVII.**   Christianismus.

The only begotten eternal *Son of God*, 3. | Unigenitus æternus *Dei Filius*, 3.

being promised to
our first Parents in Para-
dise, at the last being conceived by the *Holy Ghost*,
in the most Holy Womb
of the *Virgin Mary*, 1. of
the royal house of *David*
and clad with humane
flesh, came into the World
at *Bethlehem* of *Judæa*,
in the extream poverty
of a *Stable*, 2.
in the fullness of time,
in the year of the world
3970, but pure from all sin,
and the name of *Jesus*
was given him,
which signifieth a *Saviour*.
When he was sprinkled
with *holy Baptism*, 4.
(the *Sacrament*
of the *new Covenant*)
by *John* his Forerunner,5.
in *Jordan*,
the most sacred *Mystery*
of the divine *Trinity*,
appear'd by the *Father's*
voice, 6. (whereby he testi-
fied that this was his *Son*)
and the *Holy Ghost* in the
shape of a *Dove*, 7. coming
down from Heaven.

From that time, being
the 30th year of his Age,
unto the fourth year, he
declared who he was, his
words and works manifest-
ing his Divinity, being
neither owned, nor enter-
tained by the *Jews*,because
of his voluntary poverty.

promissus
Protoplastis in Paradiso,
tandem con-
ceptus per *Sanctum Spirit-*
um in sanctissimo utero
Virginis Mariæ, 1.
de domo regiâ *Davidis,*
& indutus humanâ
carne, prodiit in mundum
Bethlehemæ Judæâ,
in summâ paupertate
Stabuli, 2.
impleto tempore,
Anno Mundi 3970,
sed mundus ab omni pec-
cato & nomen *Jesu*
impositum fuit ei,
quod significat *Salvatorem*.
Hic, cum imbueretur
sacro Baptismo, 4.
(*Sacramento*
novi Fœderis)
à *Johanne* præcursore suo,
5. in *Jordane* apparuit
sacratissimum *Mysterium*
Divinæ *Trinitatis,*
Patris
voce, 6. (quâ testabatur
hunc esse *Filium* suum)
& *Spiritu sancto*
in specie *Columbæ*, 7.
delabente cœlitus.

Ab eo tempore,
tricesimo anno ætatis suæ,
usque an annum quartum,
declaravit quis esset,
verbis & operibus præ se
ferentibus Divinitatem,
nec agnitus, nec acceptus
a *Judæis*, ob
voluntariam pauperatem.

He was at last taken by these (when he had first instituted the *Mystical Supper*, 8. *of his Body and Blood* for a Seal of the *new Covenant* and the remembrance of himself) carried to the *Judgment-seat of Pilate*, Governour under *Cæsar*, accused and condemned as an innocent *Lamb;* and being fastned upon a *Cross*, 9. *he dyed*, being sacrificed upon the Altar for the sins of the World.

But when he had revived by his Divine Power, he rose again the third day out of the *Grave*, 10. and forty days after being taken up from *Mount Olivet*, 11, into *Heaven*, 12. and returning thither whence he came, he vanished as it were, while the *Apostles*, 13. gazed upon him, to whom he sent his *Holy Spirit*, 14. from *Heaven*, the tenth day after his *Ascension*, and them, (being filled with his power) into the World to preach of him; being henceforth to come again to the *last Judgment*, sitting in the mean time

Captus tandem ab his (quum prius instituisset *Cœnam Mysticam*, 8. *Corporis* & *Sanguinis sui*, in Sigillum *novi Fœderis*, & sui recordationem) raptus ad *Tribunal Pilati*, Præfecti *Cæsarei*, accusatus & damnatus est *Agnus* innocentissimus; actusque in *Crucem*, 9. *mortem subiit*, immolatus in arâ pro peccatis mundi.

Sed quum revixisset Divinâ suâ Virtute, resurrexit tertia die è *Sepulchro*, 10. & post dies XL. sublatus de *Monte Oliveti*, 11. in *Cœlum*, 12. & eo rediens unde venerat, quasi evanuit, *Apostolis*, 13. aspectantibus, quibus misit *Spiritum Sanctum*, 14. de *Cœlo*, decima die post *Ascensum*, ipsos vero, (hac virtute impletos) in Mundum prædicaturos; olim rediturus ad *Judicium extremum*, interea sedens

at the *right hand*
of the Father,
and interceding for us.

 From this *Christ* we
are called *Christians*, and
are saved in him alone.

ad *dextram*
Patris,
& intercedens pro nobis.

 Ab hoc *Christo*
dicimur *Christiani*,
inque eo solo salvamur.

Mahometism.   CXLVIII.   Mahometismus.

Mahomet, 1.
a warlike Man,
invented to himself
a new Religion,
mixed with *Judaism*,
Christianity and *Gentilism*,
by the advice of a *Jew*, 2.
and an *Arian Monk*, 3.
named *Sergius*; feigning,
whilst he had the *Fit of
the Falling-sickness*,
that the *Archangel Gabriel*
and the *Holy Ghost*,
talked with him,

Mahomet, 1.
Homo bellator,
excogitabat sibi
novam Religionem,
mixtam ex *Judaismo*,
Christianismo & *Gentilismo*,
consilio *Judæi*, 2.
& *Monachi Ariani*, 3.
nomine *Sergii*; fingens,
dum laboraret *Epilepsia*,

Archangelum Gabrielem,
& *Spiritum Sanctum*,
secum colloqui,

using a *Pigeon*, 4.	adsuefaciens *Columbam*, 4.
to fetch Meat	petere Escam
out of his Ear.	ex Aure sua.
His *Followers*	*Asseclæ* ejus
refrain themselves	abstinent se
from *Wine;*	à *Vino ;*
are circumcised,	circumciduntur,
have many *Wives ;*	sunt *Polygami ;*
build *Chapels*, 5.	exstruunt *Sacella*, 5.
from the *Steeples* whereof,	de quorum *Turriculis*,
they are called to Holy	convocantur ad sacra
Service not by *Bells*,	non a *Campanis*,
but by a *Priest*, 6. they	sed a *Sacerdote*, 6.
wash themselves often, 7.	sæpius se abluunt, 7.
they deny the *Holy Trinity:*	negant *SS. Trinitatem :*
they *honour Christ*,	*Christum honorant*,
not as the *Son of God*,	non ut *Dei Filium*,
but as a great *Prophet*,	sed ut magnum *Prophetam*,
yet less than *Mahomet ;*	minorem tamen *Mahomete;*
they call their *Law*,	*Legem* suam vocant
the *Alchoran.*	*Alcoran.*

Gods Providence.   CXLIX.   Providentia Dei.

Mens States | Humanæ Sortes

are not to be attributed
to *Fortune* or *Chance*,
or the *Influence of the Stars*,
(*Comets*, 1.
indeed are wont to por-
tend no good)
but to the provident
Eye of God, 2.
and to his *governing Hand*,
3. even our *Sights*,
or *Oversights*,
or even our *Faults*.

   God hath his *Ministers*
and *Angels*, 4.
who accompany a *Man*, 5.
from his birth,
as *Guardians*,
against wicked *Spirits*,
or the *Devil*, 6.
who every minute
layeth wait for him,
to tempt
and vex him.

   Wo to the mad
Wizzards and *Witches*
who give themselves to
the *Devil*,
(being inclosed in a *Circle*, 7. calling upon him
with Charms)
they dally with him,
and fall from God !
for they shall receive their
reward with him.

non tribuendæ sunt
Fortunæ aut *Casui*,
aut *Influxui Siderum*,
(*Cometæ*, 1.
quidem solent nihil boni
portendere)
sed provido
Dei Oculo, 2.
& ejusdem *Manui rectrici*, 3.
etiam nostræ *Prudentiæ*,
vel *Imprudentiæ*,
vel etiam *Noxæ*.

   Deus habet *Ministros*
suos, & *Angelos*, 4.
qui associant se *Homini*, 5.
à nativitate ejus,
ut *Custodes*,
contra malignos *Spiritus*,
seu *Diabolum*, 6.
qui minutatim
struit insidias ei,
ad tentandum
vel vexandum.

   Væ dementibus
Magis & *Lamiis*
qui Cacodæmoni se
dedunt
(inclusi *Circulo*, 7.
eum advocantes
Incantamentis)
cum eo colludunt
& à Deo deficiunt !
nam cum illo
mercedem accipient.

The Last Judgment.   CL.   Judicium extremum.

For the *last day*
shall come
which shall raise up the
Dead. 2. with the sound of
a *Trumpet*, 1. and summon
the *Quick* with them
to the *Judgment-seat*
of *Christ Jesus*, 3.
(appearing in the Clouds)
to give an Account
of all things done.

When the *Godly* & *Elect*,4.
shall enter into life eter-
nal into the place of Bliss,
and the new *Hierusalem*, 5.

But the *Wicked*
and the *damned*, 6.
shall be thrust into *Hell*,8.
with the *Devils*, 7. to be
there tormented for ever.

Nam *dies novissima*
veniet,
quæ resuscitabit *Mortu-
os*, 2. voce *Tubæ*, 1.
& citabit *Vivos*,
cum illis
ad *Tribunal*
Jesu Christi, 3.
(apparentis in Nubibus)
ad reddendam rationem
omnium actorum.

Ubi *pii* (*justi*) & *Electi*, 4.
introibunt in vitam æter-
nam,in locum Beatitudinis
& novum *Hierosolymam*, 5.

Impii vero.
& *damnati*, 6.
cum *Cacodæmonibus*, 7. in
Gehennum, 8. detrudentur,
ibi cruciandi æternum.

The Close.   CLI.   Clausula.

Thus thou hast seen in
short, all things
that can be shewed,
and hast learned
the *chief Words*
of the *English* and *Latin*
Tongue.

Go on now
and read other good *Books*
diligently,
and thou shalt become
learned, wise, and *godly.*

Remember these things;
fear God, and call upon
him, that he may bestow
upon thee
the *Spirit of Wisdom.*

Farewell.

Ita vidisti summatim
res omnes
quæ poterunt ostendi,
& didicisti
Voces primarias
Anglicæ & *Latinæ*
Linguæ.

Perge nunc
& lege diligenter alias
bonos *Libros,*
ut fias
doctus, sapiens, & *pius.*

Memento horum ;
Deum time, & invoca
eum, ut largiatur
tibi
Spiritum Sapientiæ.

Vale.

An Index of the Titles.

AN INDEX OF THE TITLES.

AN INDEX OF THE TITLES.

AN INDEX OF THE TITLES.

Trinuni Deo Gloria.

FINIS.